Elite Performance Skills

by

Life is a Special Operation.com

Copyright © 2019 by Littlestone

All rights reserved. No part of this publication may be reproduced, distributed or transmitted in any form or by any means, without prior written permission.

Elite Performance Skills / Paperback -- 1st ed.
ISBN: 978-1-946373-04-5
$17.99 everywhere great books are sold

Macro- Table of Contents:

Greetings from the Editor in Chief
How this Book is Organized
1. Disciplines of Success — 20
2. Training & Education — 36
3. Astonishing Leadership — 42
4. A World Class Team — 54
5. Health — 59
6. Self-Economics — 70
7. Manners — 98
8. Persuasion — 112
9. Negotiations — 124
10. Security — 137

Conclusion

Table of Contents

Greetings from the Editor in Chief 17

My Business Model 17

How this Book is Organized 18

Disciplines of Success 20
1. No Excuses.. 20
2. Discipline 20
3. Self-Motivation 20
4. Focus 21
5. Say "No" 21
6. Simplify your Distractions 22
7. Visualize Success 22
8. Win Hearts and Minds 23
9. Always Exceed Expectations 23
10. Never Quit….. 23
11. But Don't Waste Your Time 24
12. Be Happy with Who you Are 24
13. You will be Pre-Judged 25
14. Hair, Grooming, Skin 25
15. Style 28

16.	Accessories Matter	28
17.	Confidence	29
18.	Humility	29
19.	The Wolf or the Sheep	29
20.	Don't Trust Anyone	30
21.	Communications and Vocabulary	30
22.	Speak Multiple Languages	31
23.	Never Interrupt	31
24.	Truth & Integrity	31
25.	Don't Talk About It, Do It	31
26.	Bad Weather & Just Bad Clothes	32
27.	Your Most Dangerous Missions	32
28.	Tactical – Operational - Strategic	33
29.	Tactical Missions with Strategic Results	33
30.	Identify your Purpose for Every Meeting	34
31.	Your Board Members	34

Training & Education 36
1. Life Long Learning / Training 36
2. Go to the Hardest Schools 37
3. Not Everyone is Elite 37
4. No All University Degrees are the Same 38
5. How to Get into Harvard 38
6. Do What You Want to Do 40

Astonishing Leadership 42
1. Set the Example 42
2. Golden Rule 42
3. Punctuality 42
4. Time Management 42
5. Energy Management 43
6. Organized 43
7. Competence...................................44
8. Admit You Are Wrong 44
9. Remember Names 44
10. Send a Hand Written Thank You 45
11. E-mail SOP 45
12. Listen..46
13. Keep your Door Open 47
14. Ask for Help................................47
15. Plan Everything...........................48
16. Time Matters 48
17. Risk Management 48
18. End state......................................49
19. Know your Operational Environment.....49
20. Rehearsals 50
21. Proprietary Planning Process 50

A World Class Team 54
1. Surround Yourself with the Best of the Best 54

2.	Leave People Behind or Pass Them By	54
3.	Be Diverse... But Not Too Diverse	55
4.	Free Yourself of Drama	55
5.	After Action Review / Lessons Learned	55
6.	Delegate / Outsource All You Can	56
7.	Let your Subordinate Elites Fail	56
8.	Isolate Yourself When Needed	57
9.	Let your Team Rise to the Occasion	57
10.	Know What Motivates Your Team	58
11.	Challenge the Team	58
12.	Genuine Interest in Others	58

Health 59

1.	No Carpet	59
2.	No Air Conditioning	59
3.	No Processed Food	60
4.	No Cold / Processed Beverages	60
5.	No Hormones	60
6.	Perfect Posture	61
7.	Sleep	62
8.	Morning Workouts	63
9.	Dieting	64
10.	The 10pm Rule	66
11.	No Snooze Alarm	66
12.	Take a Real Vacation	68

Money / Self-Economics..................................70
1. Self-Economics 70
2. Wealth Is Not Income 71
3. Build Wealth – Don't Spend It 71
4. Use Your Salary to Build Wealth 72
5. Budget 72
6. Live Under Your Budget...................73
7. Marry A Frugal Spouse.....................73
8. Pocket Money 74
9. Cigarettes & Coffee 75
10. Cell Phones Are Money Pits 75
11. Pay Cash for Everything 76
12. Beware: Credit Cards 76
13. Beware: Taxes Hurt 77
14. Beware: Banks Are Criminals..........78
15. Beware: Colleges & Universities 79
16. Don't Try to Impress Your Neighbors......80
17. Emergency Savings Account 81
18. Get Rid of Debt................................82
19. Own the House You are Living In ...82
20. Buy A Used Car 83
21. Disaster Proof Your Life (a Will) 84
22. Disaster Proof Your Life (Insurance)........84
23. Buy Assets – Not Liabilities 86

24.	Earn Passive Income	86
25.	Start A Small Business	87
26.	Start a Big Business	88
27.	You Must Find Good Employees	88
28.	Get A Great Assistant	88
29.	Marketing	89
30.	Look for Opportunities	90
31.	Work Effectively	90
32.	Don't Procrastinate	91
33.	Go Into The Right Business	91
34.	Give Value / "The Law of Effection"	91
35.	Knowledge	92
36.	Persistence	92
37.	Amazing Customers Service	93
38.	Investments	93
39.	How Much to Invest	93
40.	Don't Invest if you Don't Understand	94
41.	Get a Fiduciary not a Financial Planner	95
42.	Index Funds	95
43.	Automate Savings & Investments	96
44.	Minimize Fees	96
45.	Roth IRA	96
46.	Roth 401(k)	97

Manners 98
1. Definition / History 98
2. Golden Rule 98
3. Say Please & Thank You 99
4. Asking to Help 99
5. Authenticity 99
6. Remember Names 100
7. Punctuality 100
8. Greetings 100
9. Introductions 100
10. Never Interrupt 101
11. Listening 101
12. Ask if it is Convenient for Others 101
13. Communications and Vocabulary 102
14. Hand Shakes 102
15. Eye Contact 102
16. Cell Phones 102
17. Holding Doors 103
18. Walking in the Street 103
19. Vehicles 104
20. Public Places 104
21. Invitations to Someone's House 104
22. Restaurants 105
23. Dining Table 106

24.	Posture	107
25.	Style & Grooming	107
26.	Always Exceed Expectations	107
27.	Send a Hand Written Thank You	108
28.	E-mail SOP	108
29.	Ask for Help	109
30.	Wash Hands	110
31.	Scratching	110
32.	Snorting or Spitting	110
33.	Confidence	110
34.	Humility	110
35.	Truth & Integrity	111

Persuasion 112

1.	Persuasion -v- Manipulation	112
2.	Elements of Persuasive Design	112
3.	Authenticity / Winning Hearts and Minds	113
4.	KIS: Keep is Simple	113
5.	Know your Purpose	113
6.	Consider and Know your Audience	114
7.	Have a Goal for Every Meeting	114
8.	Emotional Intelligence	115
9.	Don't Waste Your Time	115
10.	Rehearse then Re-Rehearse	116

Tools / Techniques of persuasion 116

1.	Appeal to Emotions	116
2.	Data and Statistics	116
3.	Authority	116
4.	Time / Resources are Scare	117
5.	Multi-Media	117
6.	Language and Vocabulary	117
7.	I'm Just Like You (Language / Accent)	117
8.	I'm Just Like You (Situation)	117
9.	Ask Great Questions	118
10.	Body Language / Non-Verbal's	118
11.	Shock Factor	118
12.	Assume the Moral High-Ground	118
13.	Ultimate Good	118
14.	Illustrations	119
15.	Analogies	119
16.	Metaphors	119
17.	Similes	120
18.	Humor	120
19.	Likability	120
20.	Remember Names	120
21.	Give a Lot	121
22.	Foot in the Door	121
23.	Say "Yes"	121
24.	Pride	121
25.	Repetition	122

26. Persistence..122
27. Story Telling..122
28. Peer Pressure / Conformity 122
29. Duty..122
30. Fear...122
31. Take the Other Side.................................123
32. Alliterations / Rhymes.............................123

Negotiations 124
Lessons Learned from Harvard............................124
Lessons Learned from Life 124
Elements of Negotiation..125
1. Pre-Negotiation Phase 125
2. Negotiation Phase.....................................125
3. Post-Negotiation Phase 126
4. Define your Objective 127
5. Define your Minimum / Maximum 127
6. Currency & Value Come in Many Forms ...127
7. Know and Understand all Parties 128
8. ZOPA 129
9. BATNA 130
10. Ethics...130
11. Establish Negotiation Rules 131
12. Emotional Intelligence 131
13. Body Language / Non-Verbals.................132

| 14. | Obstacles and Dead Ends | 132 |
| 15. | Rehearse. Then Re-Rehearse | 132 |

Negotiation Tools / Techniques 133

1.	Anchor Points	133
2.	High Initial Offer	133
3.	Split the Difference	133
4.	Role Play	134
5.	Build Coalition	134
6.	Let Other Parties Fight It Out	134
7.	Appeal to Emotions	134
8.	Use Data and Statistics	135
9.	Time / Resources are Scare	135
10.	Bureaucracy	135
11.	Shock Factor	135
12.	Take the Other Side	136
13.	Ultimate Good / Fairness	136
14.	Give Away / Concede	136
15.	Look for the Win / Win	136

Security 137

1.	Physical Self Defense	137
2.	Yell for Help	138
3.	The 120% Rule	138
4.	Go for the Vulnerable Parts	139
5.	Upgrade Your Situation	139

6.	Avoid Bad Places	139
7.	Low Profile	140
8.	Don't Flash Your Wealth	140
9.	The 2 Man Rule	140
10.	The 10PM Rule	141
11.	Safety Gear	141
12.	Cyber Security	142
13.	Antivirus	142
14.	Back Up Your Data	143
15.	Passwords	143
16.	VPN	143
17.	Social Media Privacy	144
18.	Car Security	144
19.	House Security	144
20.	Smart Phone Security	145
21.	Emergency Fund	146
22.	Emergency Kit for the Car	147
23.	Emergency Kit for the House	147
24.	Intelligence	148
25.	Counterintelligence	148

Conclusion: Do What You Know is Right 150

Greetings from the Editor in Chief

My name is Christopher Littlestone and I am a retired U.S. Army Special Forces (Green Beret) Lieutenant Colonel who has been an Elite professional for over twenty years. I have a Master's Degree from Harvard and am a Special Forces Combat Diver, an Airborne Ranger, and a decorated war veteran who has spent over ten years serving outside of the United States.

I have taken "lessons learned" from my unique career and amazing life, both the good and the bad, and made them available to you. Everything I say is tried and true. Everyone, young or old, civilian or military, already Elite or soon-to-become Elite, can learn and benefit from the "best practices" and "standard procedures" of Special Operations & Elite Performers.

My Business Model

"Create Value & Give"

Because millions of people pay their consultants, lawyers, psychologists, exercise trainers, and life coaches $100 an hour or more for every consultation, they should gladly pay $17.99 to get an exceptionally insightful and life-changing product from a world-class performer.

How this Book is Organized

<u>Full Range of Topics:</u> Because this is a book, not a face-to-face consultation where we can get to work on exactly what you need to learn, I am going to list every Success Skill in my repertoire. Benefit from all of them, but use the "Table of Contents" to focus yourself. There are five paragraphs which I have published twice. This is because some people will not read the entire book but will only read certain sections.

<u>Principles not Stories:</u> This book captures the ideas, principles, and concepts of Elite Performance. It doesn't tell feel-good stories about Elite Performance. I have written this book to correspond with the way I learn. I don't need a 350-page book of feel-good stories to learn the seven habits of highly effective people. I need seven sentences to tell me what they are. I am smart enough to figure the rest out. The fluff simply slows me down. Feel-good books sell millions of copies to people who want to feel good. I don't want you to <u>feel</u> good, I want you to <u>be</u> good. My goal is nothing short of helping you to become the best of the best, an Elite Performer.

<u>The Figurative Mountain:</u> "Climbing the mountain" is the best parable or illustration I can use to describe your challenge or goal. Perhaps "climbing the mountain" means starting that business you have always wanted to start. Perhaps it means getting promoted at work, being a better stay-at-home

mother, or simply running a marathon faster. Elite Performers make a difference in the world, they accomplish goals, they climb mountains.

<u>Valley Dwellers:</u> This is the name I give to people who live in the valley. They have a view of the mountain every day, but never have the courage to leave the valley and climb the mountain.

<u>Don't Underestimate the Power of Reading:</u> Some of my classes at Harvard required hundreds of pages of reading every day. Yes, the Harvard professors are the best in the world and they ask the hard questions, draw out answers, and find links between what you know and what you have read. But simply doing the reading was 90% of the work. So, read, read, and read … to increase your knowledge base.

<u>Bullet Comments:</u> To save you time and energy, I am going to use a lot of bullets. Bullets are logically arranged to expedite learning.

<u>*Case Studies / War Stories (marked with italics):*</u> Read a case study or an example from my life to further drive home the point. Or simply skip it and move to the next Performance Skill.

<u>Study, Rehearse, Master:</u> Simply reading this book is not going to be enough. You must deliberately study, rehearse, and master these Elite Performance Skills.

Disciplines of Success

1. No Excuses

By the time you are an adult, your life is your own fault. There is no one to blame but yourself. Although not everyone can get to the top of the mountain, there is a lot of room up here. The air is cleaner, and the view is magnificent. Most people choose to remain in the valley with the majority of other people. If you really want to get to the top of the mountain, then it is up to you to plan, train, rehearse, and then climb your way to the top. No one can do it for you.

2. Discipline

Discipline is essential for finishing what you started and accomplishing preset goals. Only discipline helps you stay resolved when you are discouraged, challenged, and literally or figuratively cold, wet, hungry, or tired. You can never climb to the top of the mountain without discipline.

3. Self-Motivation

Elite performers don't need someone to yell at them to motivate them. There is no cheering at the top of the mountain. They simply do it because they know that what they are doing is worth the effort.

4. Focus

Staying focused on the tasks at hand while freeing yourself from distraction is a requirement for mission accomplishment. Easily distracted people never become Elite Performers. They spend most of their free time in front of the television being distracted or entertained. Lazy people never become Elite Performers because they can never stay focused on their mission. Elite Performers prioritize what to focus on and what to ignore. Most things are ignorable, for example, the hyperbole in the news, the nonsense in the gossip circle, or the negativity of your colleagues.

While training during the Special Forces Advanced Urban Combat Course, the instructors continually detonate hand grenade simulators and other explosives and pyrotechnics to the point that you are no longer distracted by explosions and loud noises. Tuning out the explosions and the noises of war helps special operators stay focused on their mission. Tuning out the negative voices of their environment or workplace helps Elite Performers accomplish their goals.

5. Say "No"

An Elite Performer must be able to say "no." You can be nice about it, but it is essential that you learn to say no. "No, I won't let you drag me down the mountain." "No, I will not carry that for you up the mountain." "No, I will not stay here in the valley forever." "Yes, I will climb that mountain."

6. Simplify Your Distractions

When hiking to the top of the mountain, you must carefully and selectively prioritize and choose every single piece of gear in your backpack: rain jacket, food, first aid kit, and compass. Now is not the time to bring dead weight. Now is not the time to drag a net. You must be agile, efficient, and focused. Stop wasting your precious time with distractions. When appropriate, turn off the television, stop listening to the radio, and put away your cell phone. Consider checking your e-mail once a day rather than twenty times a day. Consider getting rid of a few of your hobbies or saying "No" to a "drama queen" friend to free up some time and energy.

7. Visualize Success

Elite Performers visual their success prior to their best performances. Relax somewhere comfortable. Close your eyes. Walk yourself through your performance. This can be sped up or slowed down based upon time available. Think of it as a mental rehearsal.

A concert pianist takes a few minutes before a performance to play the song on an imaginary keyboard in her dressing room. She triggers each finger muscle and nerve, listens to each note, feels the music. Five minutes later, she flawlessly performs the same song to a crown of thousands.

8. Win Hearts and Minds

When fighting a war or competing in the marketplace, it is essential that you win the hearts and minds of the populace. You must show the people that you care for them and are there for them. Authenticity is a must. Honesty and integrity are essential. Valley inhabitants are not dumb. They can spot an inauthentic faker a mile away.

9. Always Exceed Expectations

If you are expected to deliver "one," exceed expectations and deliver "two." If you are required to give a presentation at the office, give the presentation, but exceed expectations and prepare snacks and beverages. By always exceeding expectations, you will earn the reputation of an overachiever and become the favorite.

10. Never Quit …

Elite Performers never quit. No excuses. Finish what you start.

11. But Don't Waste Your Time

Elite Performers are productive. Yes, they start what they finish. But they also recognize that some things are a waste of time. If you have four product lines at work, but only two of them are making money, then stop wasting your time with the two failed product lines and energize the good product lines to make them even more productive. If you are slow or average at a certain task, then outsource it to a professional who can do it better, cheaper, and in less time.

12. Be Happy with Who You Are

The modern-day preoccupation with body image is absolutely out of control. Sex sells. Skinny is awesome. Image is everything. This is all wrong. This is not the way it is supposed to be. Please don't let the evil fashion industry manipulate you into being unhealthy. Did you know that some "supermodels" starve themselves, are anorexic, have surgery upon surgery, and even go through terrible measures to break and stretch their bones to make themselves taller? This is unnatural. Worshipping the fashion world's images is not healthy, and Elite Performers are healthy.

We can't fight genetics. Some of us are born big, others small. Some men can put on muscle easily and others will be skinny their entire lives. The key is to take care of what you were given and to be the healthiest you possibly can be.

13. You will be Pre-Judged by a Superficial World

We do not live in a perfect world where we are judged by our heart, our abilities and our potential. We live in a superficial world where we are judged by first impressions and how we look. Elite Performers use this to our advantage by make sure we always make a good first impression. We are groomed and well dressed. We have manners. We stay physically fit. Dress and look the part. Be the part. And, as discussed in the previous Elite Performance attribute, we don't fight our own genetics, we are healthy, and we are happy with who we are.

14. Hair, Grooming, Skin

★ Hair tips for men: Out of control hair is "cool," but not a trademark of elite bankers. Having an appropriate and professional haircut with immaculate styling is absolutely a way to nail your first impression. Don't be lazy, use some product. But make sure it is a good product. Male baldness is 50% genetics and 50% your own fault. If you are already bald, it is too late. All we can say is do not make a comb-over.

★ If you are not bald, then do the following to keep and maintain healthy hair into old age: Always use the best shampoo and best conditioner to keep your hair healthy. Wash your hair no more than twice a week to ensure that the oil in your scalp isn't washed away. This is the main cause of baldness. Blow dry your hair with low heat. Never dye your hair. Enjoy your gray hair, if you have it, and use it to your advantage to look wiser.

★ Hair tips for women: Long hair is "beautiful" and a short hairstyle is "cute." Would you rather be beautiful or cute? The answer is obvious. Keep your hair as long as you can. Wear an updo if you need to make a power play or want to be elegant. Don't dye your hair. Natural color is the new blond. Enjoy your gray hair, if you have it, and use it to your advantage to look wiser.

★ Beards: Have you ever noticed that only motorcycle gang members, Taliban, and "rockabillies" have super long beards? Your banker is clean-cut. You lawyer is clean-cut. Your CEO is clean-cut.

★ Grooming: Cut and maintain your eyebrows and facial hair. Take care of your toenails so you can walk pain-free. Take care of your fingernails so you can make a good impression. Excessively long fingernails are trashy. Good-looking fingernails are a sign of refinement and discipline. Chewed fingernails are the sign of someone preoccupied and worried about themselves.

★ Skincare: Skincare is important for both men and women. Most women know how to take care of their skin, but it is easy to spot a man who takes care of his skin. Taking care of your skin is healthy, and it makes you look and feel good. In the morning, everyone should put on a good moisturizer. Women should only use high-quality makeup. Makeup should be fun and used to underline beauty. Makeup should never be a requirement. And makeup should never be caked on. At the end of your day, it is essential that you wash your face with a moisture-rich cleanser. Then, apply a serum to give vitamins to your dermis and hypodermis (inner skin). And finish it all off with a night cream to moisturize your epidermis (outer skin). If you use a drying soap, then your serum and moisturizer only gives moisture to the epidermis. But if you use a moisturizing soap, then your epidermis is moisturized and your serum can help heal and give vitamins to your inner skin. Use sunscreen and wear a hat.

15. Style

The nicer you are dressed, the better you feel. Better to own only a few, well-fitting essentials than to have a closet full of poorly fitting average clothes. Dress the part. Make a good impression. Women, be elegant and modest. Men, don't be dull in your style. You must learn how to accessorize. Remember, style is a key ingredient in the total package.

A millionaire with exceptional style was forced to shop at Walmart. He bought blue jeans, a white dress shirt, matching shoes and belt, a scarf, aviator sunglasses, and hair gel. He looked like a million dollars, but spent $50.

16. Accessories Matter

Use accessories to upgrade any outfit. Men, for example, buy a nice watch, a unique wallet, wear a scarf, use a pocket square, put on some colorful shoe laces, and wear a blazer when you are in jeans. Women, wear a nice scarf, have a great pair of shoes, and carry a fantastic handbag. When it comes to jewelry, less is more. But make sure that what you have is good quality. Better to have one nice ring, one nice handbag, and one nice winter jacket than to have a closet full of average accessories. Classics and quality are built to last and never go out of style.

17. Confidence

Confidence is always valued. Arrogance is never appreciated. Real confidence comes from the quiet certainty of one's abilities and competencies. False confidence comes from an overrated and unrealistic opinion of oneself and one's skills. Elite Performers are all confident. But they are not Elite Performers because they are confident … they are confident because they are Elite Performers. Their skills and abilities make them confident. Skills and abilities come before confidence.

18. Humility

Humility is an essential attribute of Elite Performers and is a result of the before mentioned quiet certainty of one's abilities and competencies. Elite Performers like to let their actions speak for themselves. They stay and remain grounded, humble.

19. The Wolf or the Sheep

One of my favorite moments in my Special Forces training was the "Wolf Speech" from our eccentric hand-to-hand combat instructor. He basically said Special Forces Operators are like wolves and that everyone else in the world is a sheep. Wolves eat sheep. No matter how big the sheep is, a wolf can always eat the sheep. The sheep doesn't scare the wolf, and the sheep certainly doesn't eat the wolf. Although Elite Performers are not wolves, we can learn from this illustration. Elite Performers dominate. Village dwellers (those who refuse to climb the mountain) and their negativity don't scare Elite Performers. When village dwellers tell Elite Performers that climbing the mountain is impossible or dangerous, the Elite Performer is not scared.

20. Don't Trust Anyone

Because there is a lot of selfishness out there, you need to always be on your guard. You wear your seatbelt not because you don't trust your own driving skills, but because you don't trust the driving skills of the other drivers out there. Safeguard your industrial secrets and plans. Don't talk about your mission until you have completed it. Corporate spies exist. Evil and vindictive employees exist. Always protect yourself.

21. Communications and Vocabulary

World class performers are effective communicators. They know proper grammar and use languages elegantly. They know how to use and how to read body language and other nonverbal communications. Cussing and vulgarity are never acceptable.

22. Speak Multiple Languages

World class performers learn, speak, and master languages … multiple languages. If traveling to a foreign land, they at least learn how to say *thank you* and *please* in the native language. If working in a foreign land, they learn and master the language. They know the language of their forefathers and teach these languages to their kids.

23. Never Interrupt

Let others talk, and actually listen to them. Cutting people off, ignoring them, not letting someone finish what they want to say, or not paying attention because you are formulating what you are going to say next are ways to burn bridges, destroy rapport, or lose hearts and minds. Elite Performers listen to others and show respect by not interrupting.

24. Truth & Integrity

The truth will set you free. Elite Performers don't have time for tangents or lies. They only tell the truth. Elite humans have integrity and respect themselves and others.

25. Don't Talk About It, Do It

Talk is cheap. Results and actions speak louder than words. Don't tell people what a big feat you are going to do until you do it. Elite Performers are not braggarts, they don't look at themselves in the mirror all day, flexing their own muscles. They plan something, train for it, and accomplish it. I would be a rich man if I had a dollar for every time someone told me that they were going to become a Green Beret. I always tell them, "Don't tell me, get out there and do it."

26. There is No Such Thing as Bad Weather, Just Bad Clothes

When failure is not an option, you can't stop and wait for the weather to get better. Dress appropriately and get to work. Train in the cold; walk to work in the rain. Be safe, but don't let the weather prevent you from experiencing life.

27. Do Your Most Dangerous Mission in the Rain at Night

Special Forces are taught to do their most dangerous missions on a rainy night. Human nature tells us that people let their guards down when the weather is bad. Even a terrorist would rather stay inside on a rainy night. "Yeah, I just looked out the window and everything seems safe" are their famous last words. Take advantage of suboptimal circumstances, weather, or environments to make your move.

28. Tactical – Operational – Strategic

Special Operations are conducted at the Tactical, Operational, and Strategic levels. Life is the same. Tactical level work is done at the lowest level, by the worker, the soldier, the employee. This is the easiest type of work. Although tactical work is essential, those who can do it are plentiful. I can train almost any man in the world to be a good employee. But I can't train everyone to understand the bigger picture. Operational work is done at a higher level, with oversight and perspective. Fewer people are able to perform at this level. These are managers. The highest level of performance is at the strategic level, which is for those who think globally, holistically. They connect the dots and see potential. Although Elite Performers should know how to work at the tactical level, they must function best at the strategic level.

29. Treat Every Tactical Mission as if it Had Strategic Results

Special Operations conduct surgical (tactical) missions which have global (strategic) results. Because these missions are so important, and failure is not an option, they are planned and rehearsed and have the best resources to such an extent that failure is almost impossible. Similarly, failure is not an option for an Elite Performer. So, all their operations, meetings, and briefings are planned and rehearsed, and they gather their resources to such an extent that failure is almost impossible.

30. Identify Your Purpose for Every Meeting

Purposeless meetings are a waste of your precious time and energy, so stop them or stop going to them. If you do go to a meeting, know what you want to do or accomplish before every meeting starts. For example, "The goal of this meeting is to convince the Ambassador that we can accomplish this counter drug mission and that she should let us do it." Or "The goal of this meeting is to introduce our product to the customer and give them literature about how wonderful it is. We will wait two weeks and then ask them to purchase our product during our next meeting with them at their headquarters."

31. Your Board Members may be Your Biggest Enemies

Sadly, your "Generals" or "Board Members" may be your biggest enemies. This is why most Elite Performers work for themselves. It takes thirty years to become a Senior General. So, a General relies upon tactical expertise he gained decades ago. For sure, he is out of date with modern capabilities, procedures, technology, and capabilities, slowing down the process and endangering your mission.

A young Special Forces Officer speaks Arabic, uses night vision goggles, has thermal optics and scopes on his rifle, blends in with the people, communicates securely via unconventional and conventional methods, has a Master's Degree from a reputable university, and has spent half his career in combat in a third-world country. A Senior General speaks only English, spent the first twenty years of his career planning to fight tank versus tank against nations that are now our NATO allies in Eastern Europe. His career highlights were training rotations, and his first combat tour was when he was fifty years old. He is a dinosaur. No wonder the United States wins every battle but has lost every war since Vietnam.

Elite Performers ensure that their business model is appropriate for today's operational environment and that their advisors and board members are competent, experienced experts, and are always relevant.

Training & Education

1. Lifelong Learning / Training

Elite Performers are always learning / training. They keep getting world class training. They read something educational or interesting every day. For example, you can subscribe to the Spanish "Word of the Day" to refine your second or third language. Subscribe to a YouTube channel that posts interesting facts. Read *National Geographic*. Study the Bible for ten minutes every day. Your brain is a muscle, and you must continue to exercise it with stimulating and interesting learning.

In the first twelve years of my Special Forces career, I spent six years in training. I was always learning or training, and then deploying. When I returned from a deployment, I would learn and train for the next deployment. And the cycle continued. The Lieutenant's Course (Basic Officer Training) is six months. The Captain's Course is seven-and-a-half months. Special Forces Training, Ranger School, Language School, Scuba School, and Survival School were about two years. The Major's Course was one year long. The Army sent me to Harvard to get a Master's in Government. I went to shooting schools, schools where they teach you how to steal cars, how to do evasive driving and racing, how to break and pick locks, chains, handcuffs ... This means I spent half of my career training and learning and half of my career doing it. Life is a Special Operation. Are you trained for it?

2. Go to the Hardest Schools

All things being equal, the victory will always go to the one who trained harder. The Ranger will always out-perform a standard infantryman because he is accustomed to rigorous training and harsh environments. Although you can learn a lot at a public school, the Elite go to Harvard, Heidelberg, Oxford. Admission isn't a "give me." They get into those universities because they deserve to get in. But once at these hardest schools, they are forced to learn more than someone at a "normal" school could ever imagine. For example, I read more each month at Harvard than I did each year at my public university. I was valedictorian of my public university but only graduated from Harvard.

3. Not Everyone is Elite

Life isn't a soccer game for five-year-old kids where "everyone wins." Clearly there are actual winners and losers, the average and the Elite. Some are inherently better, smarter, stronger and more capable. But most of us have the potential to overcome challenges and make it to the top.

4. Not All University Degrees are the Same

Sadly, most colleges and universities these days are businesses that crank out graduates. University tuition has increased at perhaps twenty times the inflation rate, while the caliber of graduates has diminished twenty times. A Bachelor's Degree used to mean something decades ago, and now illiterate basketball players graduate with Bachelor's Degrees. Few are the American schools these days which truly care about pumping their students so full of knowledge that they are ready to explode with wisdom. Elite Performers go to those types of schools. Harvard, Heidelberg, and Oxford have been the top three universities for the past 300 hundred years. The "Guadalajara College for Video Gaming Excellence" is not going to get you a job or catapult you to greatness.

5. How to Get into Harvard

★ Perfect Score on your SAT or ACT: To get into Harvard, you must be very smart. Even though this is obvious, thousands of dumb kids apply to Harvard each year. When I say be very smart, I mean read and study and learn until you get a perfect score on your SAT or ACT. You don't have to get a perfect score on both math and verbal, but you need a perfect score in one or the other. A perfect score basically means that out of 1,000 American high school students, you are number one. If you go to a school with 500 kids and are academically number three, you are not yet qualified. By having a perfect score on your SAT and being the smartest kid per thousand, you are showing that you are smart enough to survive the academic rigors of the school. Some kids are really smart and simply take their SAT and get in the hundredth percentile. Others are not so gifted and will need two to three years of constant reading and learning and studying. So, start early. You may be number five in a thousand, but that is not good enough. Become number one.

★ Be exceptional: You can't just be smart, you must be exceptional and unique. By being exceptional as a kid, you are showing Harvard that you will be exceptional as an adult. Statistically, Elite Performers start off as Elite Kids. Playing baseball for your school league is not exceptional. Being a Boy or Girl Scout is not exceptional. Exceptional is starting a nonprofit that provided African school kids with thousands of free laptops. Exceptional is volunteering for your local Senator and being the primary writer on a piece of legislation that later became a law. Exceptional is speaking seven languages fluently and making a YouTube channel with 2,000,000 subscribers where you teach these languages for free. Average people and those who enjoy living in the valley will not make it into Harvard, let alone graduate. Only the exceptional get in.

6. Do What You Want to Do, Not Be Who You Want to Be

Because of the prestige associated with elite occupations, many people want to <u>be</u> a doctor, <u>be</u> a lawyer, or <u>be</u> a Special Forces Green Beret. But when it is time to get to work, these people don't want to <u>do</u> what doctors do, <u>do</u> what lawyers do, or <u>do</u> what Special Forces Green Berets do.

For example, many people tell me they want to be a lawyer. I tell them: "Great. So, you love to spend eighteen hours a day in a research library reading over case files. You want to micromanage your time so that you bill every six-minute increment to a different client. You want to work hard and be the brightest because justice in this world doesn't exist, and usually the best-prepared lawyer is the one who wins. If that is what you want to <u>do,</u> then go for it. But if you simply just want to <u>be</u> a lawyer, then you will flunk out of the first year of law school.

Many people tell me they want to be a Green Beret. I then tell them: "Great. So, you want to train so hard that by the time you are forty, your body is completely broken. You want to spend six months of every year away from your wife and kids in a smelly third-world country chasing the worst bad guys on Earth and watching 25% of your best friends get killed or injured. You want to wear your thirty-pound body armor and Kevlar helmet so much that you don't even notice that they are on. Because this is what Green Berets <u>do</u>."

It is important to <u>do</u> what you want to <u>do</u>. That will make you happy. <u>Being</u> something will let you down. Elite Performers <u>do</u>.

Astonishing Leadership

1. Set the Example

Elite performers perform. They don't just talk about it. They do it. They set the example for the rest of the team to follow. They use words like "us" and "we," not "I" and "me."

2. Golden Rule

"Do to others what you would want others to do to you" (Matthew 7:12). This is a good rule by which to work and live.

3. Punctuality

Being on time illustrates that you are in control of your life and schedule and shows others that you also respect their time.

4. Time Management

Time and energy are two of the greatest commodities of Elite Performers. Great leaders effectively use their time. They don't waste their time. They plan their time in accordance with their priorities. They may give email three hours a day, but give face-to-face engagements five hours a day. Based on individual personalities, they use their commute time to listen to music and relax, make less important work calls, or use it to learn another language or listen to a book. They plan family time, vacation time, fun time, fitness time, email time, leadership time, recruiting time, training time, and learning time. Elite Performers use their time wisely.

5. Energy Management

Although everyone is different and has their preferences, we all have times of the day when we have more energy and focus. We must do our most important tasks during these times of energy and focus. Some spend their best energy learning, others spend their best energy with their loved ones. Be deliberate about using your best energy for your most important tasks.

6. Organized

Elite Performers are organized. Their lives are free of literal and figurative clutter. I tell everyone to run their lives like a business. You need a proper filing system for your bills and paperwork. You need a calendar so you can plan and schedule your life. Some use a cell phone calendar program. Others use a secretary or personal assistant. Being organized makes all the difference in the world.

7. Competence

There are no shortcuts for competence. This is why Elite Performers go through the hardest training and the most difficult schools. You can't fake competence. You are either an expert or you are not. The world is full of fakers and deceivers. The world is full of people who talk about it, but never do it. Elite Performers are super competent. They know what they are talking about and doing. If you are not convinced that you have mastered your field of expertise, then keep learning. Being Elite means that you are the most competent.

8. Admit You Are Wrong

If you are wrong, admit it quickly. Don't let others point out your mistake first. Redeem your mistakes by learning from them.

9. Remember Names

You should remember almost everyone you meet. Elite Performers remember names and lives. Among other things, remembering someone's name shows that you care. You can't be a good leader if you don't remember your team members. Elite leaders do not make excuses for "not being good with names," but show people respect by remembering their names. People will notice, I promise.

10. Send a Handwritten Thank You

In today's tech-savvy world, people have forgotten their manners and how to write a nice letter. A handwritten letter is the most honored form of read communication. Sending an email is satisfactory, but for the important messages of life, take the time to write it out by hand. Always send a handwritten thank-you note when you receive a gift or an invitation. I recommend taking a few minutes each week to make a list of the people who helped you the most, the people who are working the hardest for you, or the people who need the most encouragement. Then write each one of them a quick note.

11. Email Standard Operating Procedures (SOP)

★ Email is a form of Communication / Not the Product: Many people are slaves to their emails. They must remember that email is a form of communication, not the end product. Elite Performers are Elite because they deliver Elite Performances, not because their email inbox is always empty and they have responded to every single email.

★ No Emotions: Keep all emails professional. Never get aggressive on email. If you need to confront someone, be courageous and do it face to face.

- ★ To/CC/BCC Rules: If your name is in the "To" line, then you need to read the email, and perhaps a response or some work is required. If your name is in the "CC" or "BCC" line, then the email is just for your information.
- ★ Signature Blocks: If you are communicating with someone important, then always have a professional signature block with contact information.
- ★ Keep Records: If something may get contentious, then coordinate it over email so you have a written record with dates and times.
- ★ Leadership by Email: There is no such thing as leadership by email. So, communicate via email a few hours a day at the max, then leave your desk and lead.
- ★ Pick and Choose: Ignore or delete dumb emails from dumb people. Block them. Respond to important emails and then move on.

12. Listen

Great leaders are also great listeners. They actively listen, ask engaging questions, and learn from the people around them. But they also listen to their environment. When on a patrol in enemy territory, it is recommended that every once and a while you make a "listening halt." When you freeze, you will hear nothing. But after a minute you will hear birds, animals, perhaps even a vehicle or airplane. If the birds go silent, then be careful: someone else is near. In the civilized world, it is also recommended that you listen to the sounds of your operational environment. Are your machines running well? What do your customers say? What do the bloggers say? Pay attention. Listen. Learn.

13. Keep Your Door Open

Leaving your door open at the office means that you are available and care. Be accessible to your employees and they will tell you the truth. If you are never available and always have a shut door, then your employees never have an opportunity to tell you the truth. Plus, you are sending your employees an indirect message that you are too good to listen to them. And if you are a jerk and not approachable, everyone will be afraid to tell you the truth.

14. Ask for Help

Pride comes before the fall. So, never think you are too wonderful to ask for help. Elite Leaders are always learning, growing, developing, asking questions, and asking for help. A few good questions and a point in the right direction may save you time and money.

15. Plan Everything

Elite Performers make plans for their lives. They are proactive, not reactive. They plan everything. And because nothing ever goes perfectly, according to the plan, Elite humans make contingency plans and do risk assessments / risk mitigations. The smarter and better prepared you are, the more successful you will be.

16. Time Matters

"Time" is the word that man uses to explain the power than makes things change. Time is an essential planning consideration. Events can be planned and timed in three ways.

★ Date / Time: Certain events need to happen at a specific time.
★ Sequence: Other events may need to happen in a certain order or sequence.
★ Trigger: Some events should only happen after a specific event (the trigger) has already taken place.

17. Risk Management

Risk management is a billion-dollar industry, as all insurances are based off statistical risk algorithms.

Elite planners identify risk and ways to mitigate these risks.

In Army Special Forces, we literally have to write down every single risk we face for each operation and list at least one way to mitigate each identified risk.

18. End State

You will not succeed if you don't know what the end state (goal) is. A competent and complete end state tells you (1) the overall goal of the operation, (2) the final condition / status of your team and all the good guys, and (3) the final condition / status of your opponents.

19. Know Your Operational Environment

Knowing the cultural environment and idiosyncrasies of where you will be working, planning, meeting, or briefing is an important skill. Do your research in advance. Plan ahead. If your operational environment requires taking a tour of an outside mountainous facility, then don't wear high heels. If the owner of the company you are working with likes red, then wear a red tie.

20. Rehearsals

Rehearsals are an essential step in mission accomplishment. Elite Performers rehearse everything.

Before going on a mission to capture a well-known terrorist, a Special Forces Team conducts several rehearsals, day and night. They do daytime rehearsals first, then final rehearsals at night, with night vision goggles. They rehearse getting on and off the helicopter, placing detonation charges on the door to blow it open, and calling in progress reports on the radio. They rehearse giving someone first aid and an IV in case a team member gets shot. They rehearse how to take photos of the other bad guys at the crime scene ...

Elite Performers rehearse every presentation and sales brief. They plan and rehearse being asked the hard questions. You must visualize and rehearse your most important tasks to be better prepared for success.

21. Proprietary Planning Process

My company "Life is a Special Operation" has created our own deliberate planning process to help Elite Performers make significant decisions. This process is a proprietary planning process, created through decades of observing Elite Performers make decisions, combined with a variation of the open source U.S. military planning process. When planning for a major business or personal decision, feel free to use the process listed below. By answering, writing down, and checking off each step, you will have a more thorough understanding of the problem, the situation, solutions, and the outcome.

Understanding the Situation

1. Identify the problem. (Why are you planning?)
2. Who are the "Good Guys" and what are they doing? (your family, team, business, colleagues)
3. Who are the "Bad Guys" and what are they doing? (rival business, disloyal team members, competition)
4. What assets or people do I have available to help me and what are their capabilities / costs?
5. What legal restrictions are holding us back?

Initial Planning

6. List out every challenge identified during Step 1 and Step 3.
7. Next to each challenge listed during Step 6, write out who (one of the assets from Step 2 or Step 4) will do what to neutralize this problem. Briefly describe how.

Risk Management

8. Identify risks.
9. Identify ways to mitigate each risk.

Contingency Planning

10. Identify what could go wrong along the way.
11. Identify how to get every contingency identified in Step 10 "back on track."

Make a Collective Mission Statement

12. Who
13. What
14. When
15. Where
16. Why (purpose)
17. How
18. What is the Final Goal / End State
    a. End State of the Complete Mission
    b. End State for the Good Guys
    c. End State for the Bad Guys

Write Sub Unit Mission Statements (5Ws and How for each asset used during Step 6 and Step 7)

19. Who
20. What
21. When (can be date, time, sequence, or event triggered)
22. Where
23. Why (purpose)
24. How

Communication Plan

25. How will you communicate?
26. Identify code names or passwords.

<u>Master Event Time Line</u>

27. What should be done 1st, 2nd, 3rd, ... (You can put this into a checklist or a spreadsheet. Make sure you include time for planning, time for rehearsals, and time for an after-action review.)

A World Class Team

1. Surround Yourself with the Best of the Best

Elite performers surround themselves with the best of the best. You can't make it to the top if everyone on your team is happy to live in the valley. Find, recruit, seek out, and surround yourself only with the best of the best.

2. Leave People Behind or Pass Them By

Some people need to be left behind because they are dead weight, drama queens, or incompetent. Elite Performers don't put losers on their team. As you go to the hardest schools, as you start and complete the hardest training, and as you surround yourself only with the best of the best, you are going to pass people by. You don't need to be mean or arrogant about it, but the simple fact is that there are a lot more people living in the villages than people living at the top of the mountain.

Only 18% of the soldiers who had the courage to start Special Forces training with me actually graduated with me. They quit or didn't make it. They returned home to their village. I hope they are happy, and wished them well, but I kept going and passed them by. Only the best of the best make it into Special Forces.

3. Be Diverse ... But Not Too Diverse

A homogenized team is never as effective as a diverse team. Unique perspectives and backgrounds add to the collective capabilities of the team. But when someone is too diverse or not a die-hard believer in your mission, they are a hindrance, dead weight. Never hire a "minority" just to have a "minority" on the team. Being an Elite Performer is being a minority. Simply hire the best of the best, regardless of race, color, or creed.

4. Free Yourself of Drama

Some people are simply prone to accumulate and duplicate drama. If you spend a disproportionate amount of time on a specific person, get rid of them. Life is hard enough these days; don't waste your time and energy on drama magnets or people who are constantly having financial, relationship, or family problems.

5. After Action Review / Lessons Learned

Elite Performers take time after every mission to evaluate what they did well and what they could have done better. Aspects of the mission which went well must be sustained. Aspects of the mission which could have gone better are called "lessons learned" and should be avoided or improved on, depending on the scenario of future missions.

6. Delegate / Outsource All You Can

Elite Performers delegate or outsource all they can. Delegating is giving a task to someone else on the team. Outsourcing is giving a task to someone outside the team. Delegating tasks to others frees your calendar and gives you time for more important tasks. You can't lead if your face is always buried in a task that someone else could do. Sure, you can likely do it better than they can. But if you train them and hold them accountable, then in the long run you will have more time for the more important things. Outsourcing saves time and money. Why do it yourself, when your time is worth $100 an hour, if you can outsource payroll function, video production, or editing … to a subcontractor for $25 an hour.

7. Let Your Subordinate Elites Fail

Elite Performers are more critical of themselves than anyone else. They suffer when they fail and make sure that they will never fail again. If you have a team of Elite Performers, then be assured that they will learn more from a failure than from a success. Great leaders will let their team fail during training so that they will certainly win in real life.

During Army Special Forces training, there was a phase where all the officers were put together for what I like to call "Learning by Failing." We were broken into teams of twelve officers to plan and execute various Special Operations missions. We failed at every mission we did for several months. If we made contingency plans for everything possible from "A" to "B" to "C" to "D," then the instructors would throw scenarios "E," "F" and "G" at us. The next time we would plan for "A" through "G," so the instructors would give us "H," "I" and "J." In a group of all Super Type-A Alpha Males, we were devastated every time our missions did not go as planned. But we never once repeated the same mistake.

8. Isolate Yourself When Needed

Sometimes you need to get away to an isolated place to be and stay focused. Leaving the office or having an off-site meeting is often a good idea.

When planning for a mission, it is common for a Special Forces team to go into isolation. They will lock themselves in a building, take away all cell phones and contact to the outside world, and plan a mission for one to four days nonstop. This requires logistical support (food, water, toilets, information, and intelligence), but it gives the team members the ability to very thoroughly plan and rehearse every aspect of the mission.

9. Let Your Team Rise to the Occasion

The desire to be great or important is one of the most significant motivational factors of mankind. If you have an underachiever on your team, you can label him a "loser" and he will always be a loser. If you give him the potential to be better, something to live up to, he will gladly accept his new label and rise to the occasion.

10. Know What Motivates Your Team

The best way to get someone to do something is to make them want to do it. This requires that you genuinely understand your team. You need to know them well enough to know what motivates them. Is it pride, loyalty, the money? What do they want? Knowing what your team members want will help you to find ways to make them "want" to work for you.

11. Challenge the Team

Never overlook the power of pride to keep your team performing at the highest levels. Elite Performers want to be the best. They must be challenged and exercised so they will become and remain the best. If they aren't challenged, they will become lethargic. Challenge your team to keep them performing at their highest potential.

12. Genuine Interest in Others

Elite Performers care about and are interested in other people, especially those on their team. If you are interested in another person, you listen to them, remember their name, make them feel important, and try to see things from their perspective. This will generate a healthy team environment and increase performance.

Health

Healthy is the new wealthy. Remaining healthy is essential for Elite Performance and should be one of your deliberate and prioritized goals. Below are twelve non-debatable rules for staying healthy.

1. No Carpet

Your carpet holds exponentially more dust, germs, skin fragments, animals, bacteria, and pathogens than a hardwood or tile floor. Get rid of the carpet in your house.

2. No Air-Conditioning

Your body was designed to breathe fresh air, not chemically processed and recirculated air. Open your windows and refresh the air in your house every day. Breathing processed air is not natural. Spend as much time outside as possible.

3. No Processed Food

Your body was designed to digest real food. Processed food creates an unnatural and extremely dangerous chemical cocktail in your digestive system. Fast foods and premade foods at the grocery store are the reasons so many village dwellers are fat and cancer ridden. Natural bio foods are significantly healthier.

4. No Cold / Processed Beverages

Your body was designed to digest real juices, water, and milk. A soda or processed juice with unnatural ingredients creates a dangerous chemical cocktail in your digestive system. Cold beverages destroy the flora in your stomach, making your digestive system less effective. A daily ice-cold soda is the reason so many village dwellers are fat and cancer ridden. A daily (hot) herbal tea or room temperature water / pineapple juice is significantly healthier.

5. No Hormones

Don't mess with your hormones. Your endocrine system is amazingly sophisticated and delicate. When you take a hormone or birth control pill, it desynchronizes and hinders the delicate balance of your endocrine system. It takes years to get your body back to normal. Some never return to normal. Yes, your doctor went to medical school, but he didn't design life. So, stop playing with fire and keep your body natural.

Men take steroids to be stronger or bigger. Some of these men have died as a result of steroid use. Many get depressed when they return to normal. Some go to jail. Some develop medical problems, preventing them from working for months or years. Some grow man-boobs.

Western women take so many hormones these days. Rather than dealing with a menstrual pain, which billions of other women have dealt with, they put unnatural chemicals in their bodies. Some women have died. Some are never able to have babies. Some must wait years before they can have children. Some have unhealthy babies. And some spend their entire lives chasing the exact recipe to be and feel "normal." Had they never messed with their endocrine system in the first place, they would have always been normal.

6. Perfect Posture

The incredibly vast amount of neck, shoulder, and back pain in the Western world is caused by having habitually bad posture. The body has a natural curve in the lower back which supports the weight of the upper torso and head. When you have good posture, your body can support your weight. When you slouch, the spine is flat or arched forward, placing unnecessary pressure on supporting muscles and soft tissues like cartilage and spinal discs. When you slouch at your desk, slouch in your car, slouch at the dinner table and slouch while using your computer or cell phone, you are reversing this natural curve and are making yourself more vulnerable to back, shoulder, and neck pain. *7 Steps to a Pain-Free Life: How to Rapidly Relieve Back, Neck, and Shoulder Pain* by Robin McKenzie offers greater detail and illustrates several stretches you can do to maintain back health and proper posture. Having good posture is an essential ingredient for overall body health.

7. Sleep

Sleep is an essential aspect of health. Most of us don't get as much sleep as we need. If you need an alarm to wake up, then chances are you are not getting enough sleep. Going to bed early and getting up early is more natural and makes you more productive. I have five major rules for sleep health:

★ Go to bed early and get up early. Being awake with the sun is a much more natural rhythm. You accomplish more if you are up bright and early. And generally, those who stay up very late generally spend the last several hours of the day being unproductive while watching TV.
★ Only sleep or make love in bed. Everything else you should do elsewhere. This will make your

brain associate your bed with sleep and you will fall asleep much faster. If you eat, compute, and watch TV in bed, then you associate your bed with productivity and entertainment, not restful sleep.
★ Limit the amount of stimulation you get before going to bed. If you watch TV, especially a TV with a lot of blue light, then your brain is stimulated and requires a long time, perhaps even an hour, to unwind. It is better to read a book (not on a tablet) before going to bed.
★ Don't eat anything too heavy before going to bed. This will keep your digestive system very active and may hinder your ability to fall asleep or get a good sleep.
★ Wash or replace your pillow once a month and wash your bed cover / comforter at least once a month. An unclean bed cover is a magnet for more dust, germs, skin fragments, bacteria, and pathogens.

8. Morning Workouts

A morning workout is a great way to start your day, get your blood flowing early, and wake up your metabolism for all-day calorie burning. Although Special Operators work out every single morning as they train for war, we recommend that you work out three mornings a week and take long hikes or cross-train on the weekend. I am proud to sponsor <u>Special Operation Fitness</u> - a twelve-week unconventional training program designed to shred body fat, increase cardiovascular efficiency and muscular strength, teach or reinforce essential self-defense techniques, build confidence, and increase physical and mental performance.

9. Dieting

Most Elite Performers are already fit and in good health. But in case you need some help getting there, below are some insightful and effective principles:

★ Discipline (Have discipline and eat healthy.)

★ Wisdom (Do what you already know is healthy.)

★ Goal / End State (Make a goal that is related to clothing size or body fat percentage, write it down, and maintain it for life.)

★ Planning (Make a written plan and stick to it.)

★ Self-Esteem (Be happy with who you are … but for sure, be healthy.)

★ Childhood Fatness (Fat cells are made as a child and never go away.)

- ★ Targeting Fat (You can only lose fat collectively, not target a specific body part.)
- ★ Disorders (Inappropriate beverages, chemicals, or food use is not healthy.)
- ★ Volume (Too much food or drink is unhealthy. Eat small. Drink small. Be small.)
- ★ Energy / Calories (Know where your calories come from.)
- ★ Metabolism (Train your metabolism by eating frequent, small meals.)
- ★ All Food isn't Food (Eat only "real" food.)

- ★ Organic isn't always Bio, but Bio is always Organic (Eat Bio.)
- ★ Chemical Warfare (Beware of funny chemicals in processed food.)
- ★ Salt and Electrolytes (Don't flush your salt or essential electrolytes from your system.)
- ★ Temperature (Drink cold beverages very rarely and room temperature or warm beverages often. Eat almost all your food warm.)
- ★ Time (Eat something as soon as you get up to get your metabolism started. Don't eat your last meal so late that it disrupts sleep or causes excess calories to be stored as body fat.)
- ★ Starvation Mode (Eat frequently to avoid going into "starvation mode.")

- ★ Starvation Diets (Starvation diets are terrible because they kill your metabolism.)
- ★ Frequency (Eat small meals every three hours to keep your metabolism burning on high and to prevent your body from going into starvation mode.)
- ★ Sequence (Never eat sugars [a dessert] with alcohol. Don't eat dessert with a big meal.)
- ★ Caloric Rhythm (Make a rhythm of two or three "low-calorie days" then 1 "normal-calorie day" to keep your body from going into "starvation mode.")
- ★ "Treat" Yourself Right (Indulge occasionally, but only on a "normal calories day.")

10. The 10 p.m. Rule

Nothing good ever happens away from your house after 10 p.m. Period. Stay home and remain safe. Teenagers and village dwellers hate this rule, but it is true. I am including this rule in the health chapter because you should take advantage of being home early to go to bed early.

11. No Snooze Alarm

Turn off your alarm clock, do a few stretches, then gently get out of bed and start your morning routine.

Elite Performers do not snooze and certainly do not repeatedly snooze.

★ Snoozing doesn't allow you the time to get into deep, beneficial REM sleep. Let me oversimplify the sleep cycle: A sleep cycle is usually about two hours … ninety minutes of normal sleep and thirty minutes of rapid eye movement (REM). Most people get two to four cycles of sleep a night. Two cycles make you barely functional. Four cycles are preferred. Most of the benefits of sleep come during the REM portion of the sleep cycle. The extra five to fifteen minutes a snoozer spends in bed doesn't allow them to get into REM and, therefore, is a waste of time.

★ Snoozing wastes your valuable time. A fifteen-minute snooze six days a week is ninety minutes of wasted time a week. That is 4,680 minutes or seventy-eight hours or three-and-a-quarter days a year. If you snooze during your working years from age twenty to sixty, then you waste 187,200 minutes or 3,120 hours or 130 days. Imagine what you could have accomplished in those 130 days.

12. Take a Real Vacation

Elite Performers take real vacations. They rest, relax, and reward themselves for their hard work. Whether you are rich or poor, you must go on vacations to a place where you can rest and relax. Yes, it is important to love your family and be generous, but you must return from a real vacation happier and better rested than when you left.

For the first fifteen years of my Special Forces career, I spent all my vacation time visiting family members. I would fly home to see my mom, dad and sisters. I would take care of their "to do" list, buy them Mexican food every day, take them on a shopping spree, and go running in the mountains. And when I returned to Fort Bragg, North Carolina, I was just as tired as the day I left.

A few times, I tried what was called a "staycation" where I took two weeks of time off, but stayed at home and finished all the projects I wanted to do, but never prioritized. At the end of these staycations, I was also just as tired as the day I left ... not to mention that I violated Team Rule #6 by not delegating or outsourcing my "to do" list.

After I got married, I took my wife to a five-star beach resort with an "all inclusive" food and drink package. For a week I slept in, ate world class food, and rested outside in the sun by the sea. I returned happy, tan, rested, well fed, and my joints even hurt less. That was a real vacation, a game changer.

Money / Self-Economics

1. Self-Economics

I discovered my disdain for hard-to-read economics books while getting my Master's Degree from Harvard's School of Government. I specifically remember that one of my macroeconomics textbooks cost over $300 and was bigger than a dictionary. I always thought it was a shame that the simple principles of economics were not better summarized and explained. Off-the-shelf financial advice books are much easier to read than that a Harvard Graduate School macroeconomics textbook. But still, most of these books say in 200 pages what could be summarized in five pages. So, voila, here we are. We will discuss a little microeconomics as well as a little macroeconomics. But since we are talking about you, the individual, and your family, I will call this section "Self-Economics."

Money is always a touchy subject. Most people assume they are making good financial decisions or at least doing the best they can. But this is not true. Most people are making terrible financial decisions and banks and credit card companies are exploiting them to the max. For those of you in this category, please pay attention to the next few pages. The below listed financial principles are life-changers. For those who are already making good financial decisions and for those who truly are doing the best they can, the next few pages will reinforce your good decisions and or give you insight on how to better manage your money.

2. Wealth Is Not Income

Income is how much money you take in. Most people get paid by the hour or by the month. This is also known as a salary. Wealth is the collective value of all your assets. We will discuss assets later in this book, but for now let's say that assets include the equity you have in your house, the value of your liquidatable possessions, your bank account, and the value of your businesses (if you own any). Many people have high salaries but spend every cent. They never build wealth because they waste their money buying things which depreciate. On the flip side, many people with small salaries spend their money buying things which appreciate. They are building wealth.

3. Build Wealth – Don't Spend It

It is not wise to spend all that you make. If you make a little and spend it all, you will never build wealth. If you make a lot but spend it all, you will never build wealth. The key is to build wealth with your salary, not spend your salary.

4. Use Your Salary to Build Wealth

For most people, their salary is the best mechanism they have to build wealth. Some people will have the opportunity and the courage to start their own business or businesses. But for most people, they will simply hold a job and earn a salary, which is paid hourly or monthly. The average American holding a job in 2015 made $56,500.[1] If they maintain this salary and work for forty years, they will make over $2,262,000 in their lifetime. This is pure salary, not counting compounding interest. Yet, after forty years, most families have nothing to show for it. Can you image how much money you could make if you were given $2 million to invest in real estate or the stock market?

Most people don't recognize the huge amount of money that comes to them via their salary, and they totally miss their opportunity to use it to invest and prepare for their future.[2]

5. Budget

In a world full of bankruptcies and white-collar criminals, I feel obligated to mention the obvious.

---

[1] https://www.census.gov/newsroom/press-kits/2016/income_poverty.html

[2] Although the idea of using your salary to build wealth is common sense, I first learned it from Dave Ramsey's *The Total Money Makeover*.

Elite Performers live on a budget. They write a budget and stick to it. This requires discipline and prioritization. Sadly, most people don't live on a budget. They buy things they can't afford and hope to pay for it later. The amazing American budget deficit is simply a macro reflection of the micro stupidity of our fellow citizens. Balancing a budget is almost self-explanatory. I wonder when it became commonplace to spend more than you make without going to jail or worse. (Seriously, this is a huge cultural problem that may destroy America. I can't say enough about the importance of budgeting.)

6. Live Under Your Budget

If you make $2,000 a month, budget and spend only $1,800; save the rest. If you make $200,000 a month, live off way less and be generous. You will never get into debt if you live under your budget.

7. Marry a Frugal Spouse

Being frugal is important. But it is even better if your spouse is frugal.[3] If you are frugal but your spouse is a "spend-aholic," your finances are always going to suffer. Marry someone who is also frugal

---

[3] I first read this idea in *The Millionaire Next Door*. It is common-sensical. But I want to correctly reference the originators of the idea, Thomas J. Stanley and William D. Danko.

and I promise you that you will reap the financial benefits.

8. Pocket Money

When you make your budget, be sure to include a "pocket money" system for every member of your family. Of course, you need to pay your bills, have an emergency savings account, and build wealth with your money first. But if you have money left over, then give a little "pocket money" to each of your family members. This "pocket money" is an allowance that they alone are in charge of. When your pocket money is gone, then you don't buy silly things.

Now that I am retired, and my income is significantly less, my wife gets $350 a month for pocket money. She usually goes to the hairdresser and a massage therapist once a month. She also buys either a facial cream, makeup, or a perfume each month. All of this is about $200 a month. She then saves the rest of her pocket money for big shopping events. $150 x 12 months is $1,800. You can buy a nice wardrobe each year for $1,800. One year she bought a designer handbag. The next year a designer scarf. She saved for six months and bought me a Mount Blanc fountain pen as my Army retirement gift.

9. Cigarettes & Coffee

Small purchases add up to huge amounts over time. If the average pack of cigarettes costs $6, then your pack-a-day habit will cost you $2,190 a year (365 x $6). I recommend that you quit smoking immediately. This will save your health and your marriage. "Save your health" by no longer poisoning your lungs and "save your marriage" by saving that money for a year to buy your wife a handbag from Louis Vuitton. Your addiction to your favorite coffee shop may also cost you $6 a day. Perhaps you can buy a good coffee machine at home and bring your coffee with you to work.

We have a great coffee machine at home and I average 20 cents a cup. (Can you guess what kind of handbag my wife has?)

10. Cell Phones Are Money Pits

I know many people who pay $70 a month for their amazing cell phones with unlimited data, phone calls, and text messages. Wow, $840 a year is a lot of money. Many people can afford $840 a year for their cell phones. Most people can't. It astonishes me to see people who I know are up to their eyeballs in debt walking around with thousand-dollar phones. You should never go into debt (i.e., put it on a credit card) to buy a cell phone. It would be economically more intelligent to buy last year's model for $100, get a prepaid sim card, and use free WIFI connections at home, school, a friend's house, or public hangouts. This alone can save you hundreds of dollars a year which can be used to build wealth.

11. Pay Cash for Everything

Elite Performers pay cash for everything. This includes a car and house. It is, however, acceptable to have a mortgage on your house. This is the only acceptable debt. It is never acceptable to make payments on a car. You must always pay cash for a car. If you can't afford it, then wait a year or two before you upgrade. Cars are terrible investments because they depreciate very quickly. A car should be considered a luxury, which will be almost valueless in seven years. You should pay cash for everything. This includes a television, a cell phone, furniture, or a boat.

12. Beware: A Credit Card Is Dangerous (Use It Wisely)

Elite Performers pay for everything in cash. We just said that in the previous paragraph. Cash is mostly untraceable and helps protect one's privacy. Credit cards collect information. Credit cards get undisciplined people into a lot of trouble. When used with discipline, a credit card can be practical. But please note that I said, "use it wisely," not "use them wisely." You only need one credit card to ensure that you can buy plane tickets and make hotel reservations. Elite Performers always pay their complete balance at the end of the billing cycle. You never go over budget if you pay everything in cash. Most village dwellers make investments and have credit card debt. This makes no sense. A credit card usually rips you off at 10-25% interest. Standard, reliable investments (if there are such things) make between 5-10% interest. Why make 10% on an investment while you are losing 15% on debt?

13. Beware: Taxes Hurt

Elite Performers protect their assets. Yes, we are supposed to "render to Caesar what is Caesar's" (Mark 12:17), meaning we all need to pay our taxes to compensate for our share of the government's service. And for sure, some places tax more aggressively than others. But with a little reading and research, you can legally minimize your taxes and maximize your savings.

The Triple Tax: An overachieving village dweller in Europe makes 10,000€ (euros) a month. (1st Tax) 50% of that went to federal income taxes. He was a self-claimed Catholic, so 10% of his pay was automatically transferred to the Vatican Bank. That means he only brought home 4,000€ a month. (2nd Tax) He paid 19% sales tax on everything he ever bought. (3rd Tax) He saved 300€ a month for 45 years and when he died, he left his only son his life savings of 162,000€. The inheritance tax was 35%.

This poor man paid 60% of his income to the church and to the government, paid 19% sales tax on everything he ever bought in his entire life, and was taxed 35% on everything he didn't spend while alive. The point is: Taxes are evil, so be smart about protecting your assets ... and never open a business or live in Europe.

I can't legally provide you with tax advice (because some of you will blame your tax mistakes on me). But I will say that you must learn to itemize your deductions. This will help save you money. I further recommend that you start a business. Businesses can write off a lot more taxes than individuals. You can deduct office space, business trips, business meals, transportation, etc. I recommend you look into tax rules.

14. Beware: Banks Are Criminals

Keeping your assets safe is very good. Modern-day banking practices are suspect, at best. Elite Performers are smart about who has access to their money and how to keep their money safe. Do your research and make good decisions about how to stockpile your assets and maintain access to them.

The Waiting Game: Although it takes one microsecond to wire transfer $100,000 from your account in Bank 1 to your account in Bank 2, the transaction may take up to a week. Bank 1 will initiate the transaction on Monday morning. But they won't actually *release the funds to Bank 2 until Wednesday afternoon. During those two and a half days, Bank 1 will "play" with your money, invest your money, buy and sell with your money, and profit off your money. Bank 2 receives the money Wednesday afternoon but doesn't make the funds available to you until Saturday morning. During those three days, Bank 2 will "play" with your money, invest your money, buy and sell with your money, and profit off your money. You needed that money Monday morning, but get it Saturday. They profited off your money, and all you can do is sit around and wait.*

15. Beware: Colleges & Universities Are Businesses

★ Dare I open your eyes to this fact? While a teacher may genuinely care about you and genuinely care about making you smarter, a University is a business. It must make money to survive.

★ Yes, going to college may get you a higher-paying job. But "may" is the key word.

★ Yes, you can make money from a salary of a good job. But making money through a business is the absolute best way to make a lot of money. And starting your own business doesn't require a diploma.

★ Always pay cash for higher education. If you can't afford it, don't go. It is so sad to see new graduates with $100,000 plus in college debt.

Starting your career with a debt the size of a mortgage is absolutely irrational.
★ Save and invest for college early.
★ If you didn't do what was required to get a scholarship, then go to a cheaper university. Better to be the valedictorian of your local university than graduate in debt.
★ Not all university diplomas are the same. It would be foolish to pay an exceptional price for a below-average diploma. Do your research.

As many of you know, I went to Harvard for graduate school and paid out of pocket $63 thousand a year. It killed me financially, but I graduated with zero debt and the best education in the world. Had I not saved for years, I never would have been able to pay cash for my education. I still believe that some educations are worth the money. However, most aren't. That is why I recommend going to a cheaper university and graduating higher in your class.

16. Don't Try to Impress Your Neighbors / Colleagues / Family

For my international readers, Americans have an expression: "Don't try keeping up with the Joneses." What this means is that if the Jones family buys a new house, then you must buy a new house to keep up. If the Jones family buy a new car, then you must buy a new car. If they join a country club, then you must join a country club. You must not focus on "keeping up with the Joneses." You are not the Joneses. And statistically speaking, the Joneses are broke and making bad financial decisions. You must make a good financial decision to prepare for your future rather than make bad financial decisions to impress your broke neighbors, colleagues, and family.[4]

17. Emergency Savings Account

You must have an emergency savings account. When your car needs a repair or your refrigerator dies, it is important that you pay for it in cash, out of your emergency savings account. If you don't have an emergency savings account, then you will pay for the repair or the new refrigerator with a credit card. This will only give you more debt.

I recommend that your emergency savings account is at least:
- ★ $2,000 (hotel money for a week if you must fly to a funeral)
- ★ plus $1,000 for each family member living in your household (emergency airline tickets)
- ★ plus $2,000 for each house you own (money to fix or replace an appliance)
- ★ plus $1,000 for each vehicle your family owns (major vehicle repair)

---

[4] "Keeping up with the Joneses" is a common-sense American proverb, but one which Davey Ramsey's uses in *The Total Money Makeover*.

For example, a family of five with three cars and one house has an emergency savings fund of $12,000. I hope you never have to use your emergency fund, but statistically speaking, you will one day need to fly the entire family home for a funeral.

18. Get Rid of Debt

Hopefully you don't have any debt and can skip to the next paragraph. But if you are like most Americans, then you have a lot of credit card debt.

You must pay off your debts. If you have multiple debts, then you should pay off the debt with the highest interest rate first.

19. Own the House You are Living In

Everyone needs a place to live. So, rather than renting a place for twenty years, buy it and build equity. If you have a small salary, buy a small house. If you have a large salary, buy a medium house. And if you have a huge salary and a huge family, then buy a large house. If you have made some dumb financial decisions previously and can't get a mortgage, then start making good decisions now and apply for your mortgage in a few more years. Beware of some markets, which are terribly inflated … but for the most part, you should always own where you are living.

Pay your mortgage off early. I recommend one of three techniques:
- ★ Get a 15-year mortgage, not a 20- or 30-year mortgage.
- ★ Pay a 13th house payment each year directly towards the principal.
- ★ Pay your mortgage payment plus next month's principal every month.[5] This means you make the principal payment twice every month, i.e., your $200,000 mortgage cost you 30 years and $1,100 a month. Only $250 of your first payments pay the principal. The rest is interest. Pay your $1,100 every month and pay $250 extra a month. You will pay off your house years earlier.

20. Buy a Used Car

Buy a three-to-five-year-old car so someone else pays the initial depreciation. Because a car depreciates the second you drive it off the car lot, it is never a good idea to buy a new car. But once a car has quickly depreciated a few years, the depreciation rate slows down. This is why I recommend that you buy a three-to-five-year-old vehicle.

Don't forget that you should only pay cash for a vehicle. If you can't afford to pay cash for a nice car, then drive a safe "junker" while you save money. A

---

[5] I first learned this great idea from Tony Robbin's *Money: Master the Game*. So I want to give him credit.

vehicle is a privilege, not a right. It is transportation, not your identity. Pay cash for your three-to-five-year-old vehicle.

21. Disaster-Proof Your Life Through A Will

Make a "Last Will & Testament" and a "Medical Power of Attorney." In the terrible event of a disastrous medical problem or death, your family will know what to do. Don't do it for yourself. Do it for them. Medical disasters and death are terrible times. Die well by making it easy for those you leave behind.

I have seen so many people die terribly. Because they weren't loving enough or were too cheap or lazy to make a will, their family members suffered and fought over many medical, burial, funeral, and estate decisions.

22. Disaster-Proof Your Life Through Insurance

★ <u>Health:</u> This is essential. You must be able to pay for your medical expenses.
★ <u>Homeowner's:</u> Protect yourself in case something happens to your house. If you don't have a house but are renting, then please protect yourself via renter's insurance.

- ★ Disability & Long-Term Care Insurances are inexpensive, but can make a huge difference if you are ever disabled or have a long-term health care issue. *My last consulting job before publishing this book gave me coverage for hundreds of thousands of dollars of disability and long-term care insurance. It cost only $6 a month.*
- ★ Life: There are a lot of variations of life insurance out there. I don't recommend life insurance that doubles as an investment. I recommend term life insurance until you are about 60. After 60, term life insurance is possible, but gets more expensive. And hopefully, after 60, your family is self-sufficient and/or living from your retirement in a paid-off house.
    - ★ Example 1: A 30-year-old healthy male (nonsmoker) will pay about $45 a month for 30 years for $500,000 term life insurance. If he dies at 31 years old, he paid in $540, but his spouse gets $500,000. If he dies at age 59, he paid in $15,660 but his spouse gets $500,000. Either way, it is a win.
    - ★ Example 2: A 45-year-old healthy male (nonsmoker) will pay about $115 a month for 30 years for $500,000 Term Life Insurance. If he dies at 46 years old,

he paid in $1,380, but his spouse gets $500,000. If he dies at age 74, he paid in $40,020, but his spouse gets $500,000. Either way, it is a win.

23. Buy Assets – Not Liabilities

Smart people buy assets. Assets appreciate over time and put money in your pocket. Assets include real estate, apartment buildings, storage units, businesses, and investments in stocks, bonds, and funds.

Wasteful people buy liabilities. Liabilities take money out of your pocket. Liabilities include rental contracts, leasing cars, $1,000 cell phones, awesome TVs …

24. Earn Passive Income

The best source of wealth is from passive income. Passive income is money earned without you actively working for it. "Passive income" includes investments, stocks, bonds, T-bills, money markets, mutual funds, owning mortgages and other assets that appreciate in value and can be liquidated for cash, rental real estate, royalties from a book, music or software, licensing your ideas, becoming a franchisor, owning vendor machines, and owning storage units.[6]

As I said earlier, most people will make money through their salary. This is an active income, which exchanges money for time. It is possible to earn a passive income using some of the above listed sources as a private person. But for the best results, passive income sources come through small businesses. This leads us to my next point.

25. Start a Small Business

The best way to make a lot of money is to own your own business. This is obvious. You can't become a billionaire working nine to five for your local employer. But you can become a billionaire if you own a business that provides amazing goods and services to millions of people. Not everyone has the vision to own a company that provides amazing goods and services to millions of people. However, almost everyone can own a small business that provides small goods and small services to a small number of people. And this is why I recommend that everyone start a small business.

Starting a business is easy. Depending on where you live, it takes a few minutes of paperwork and a few hundred dollars. Even if you have a small business,

---

[6] This list of passive income sources comes from T. Harv Ecker's book, *The Secrets of the Millionaire Mind*.

you may be able to hire good employees and work yourself out of a job. Then you earn a passive income from this small business.

But if you have a rental property, then you absolutely must start a rental property company. Businesses have unique tax write-offs, which will save you a lot of money.

26. Start a Big Business

For those of you who have a bigger vision for a business than simply providing small goods and services, or having a rental property company, you are likely going to need to control a large and complex business. If your goal is to "Go Big," then you must pay attention to the next few ideas to be successful.

27. You Must Find Good Employees

A bad employee will ruin your business, perhaps your life. Hiring good people will make or break your organization. Creative people rarely need to be motivated. Hire someone who loves to work and who loves your business.

28. Get a Great Assistant

Donald Trump said in his book *How to Get Rich* that he gets 1,250 calls a week. How does he stay organized? The answer is simple. He has a great assistant. Two hundred phone calls a day is a lot of work. Which calls should he take? Who is his priority? Having a good assistant can help you to stay focused on making decisions, steering the ship, and leading your business.

29. Marketing

Create a name for yourself or your business and make sure you market it. Smart business owners are willing to promote themselves, their value and their businesses. Unsuccessful business owners think negatively about selling and promoting.[7] Some people feel that promotion is beneath them.

Imagine that you found the cure for cancer and put it in a pill that costs only $10. Everyone in the world would buy one. You would be a billionaire. But if no one knew about your cancer prophylactic, then no one would buy it and your company would go bankrupt. Marketing is essential for a successful business.

In his book *Rich Dad, Poor Dad*, Robert Kiyosaki tells an insightful story about a talented journalist with a master's in English who was an excellent writer and who wanted to be a bestselling author.

---

[7] This is a common-sense idea reinforced in Kiyosaki's *Rich Dad, Poor Dad*, Ecker's *The Secret of the Millionaire's Mind* and DeMarco's *The Millionaire Fastlane*.

She asked Kiyosaki for advice. He said she should go to marketing courses to learn how to sell her writings. She got mad and walked out, saying: "I have a master's degree in English. Why would I go to school to learn to be a salesperson? I hate salespeople. All they want is money." Kiyosaki showed her the top of his book and pointed out that it says "best-seller," not "best-writer." You must not be afraid to sell yourself and your products.

Remember that marketing is about your customers, not you. If you like red, but your customers like blue, your product better be blue.

30. Look for Opportunities

Be vigilant for opportunities. You can't look around for opportunities if your eyes are focused on your television. Turn off your TV and get to work.

31. Work Effectively

If you put 100% of your focus and effort into each activity, then you will significantly increase your probability for success. This is the difference between a Mercedes and a Chevy. The American assembly line worker is focused on tonight's football game and drinking beer with his buddies. "Herman the German" says, "I define my life by ze precision and perfection of my werk." The American does a good job, no doubt. But the German culture teaches that the way Herman perfectly assembles his car reflects the integrity of his life.

32. Don't Procrastinate

Time is precious. Don't let it slip away. What is done today is done. Elite Performers don't procrastinate. They plan, prioritize, and do each day everything which needs to be done that day.

33. Go Into The Right Business

If you can't sing or play an instrument, then you should not join a band. If you have no agility or muscles, don't be an athlete. Someone who hates to cook should never become a pastry chef. Although you can succeed at anything, success is easier when you are in a business you enjoy or one in which you have talent.[8]

34. Give Value / "The Law of Effection"

Everyone is talking about giving value these days. M.J. DeMarco's book *The Millionaire Fastlane* describes it the best. He calls "giving value" the "Law of Effection." If you "affect" or impact millions, you will make millions. Many people get mad at the overpaid athlete … you know, the guy that can

---

[8] Although this idea is common sense, it is also listed in Wattles' *The Science of Getting Rich*.

barely read, yet makes millions of dollars throwing a little ball around a grassy field. But the reason he gets paid millions is because he affects millions. Every Sunday, millions of people religiously watch him play on TV. Millions of people buy the athletic clothing he endorses. And tens of thousands of people pay for a $50 ticket to the stadium where they also buy $20 worth of snacks. That guy is a money-making machine. He affects millions, so he gets paid millions.

35. Knowledge

A successful business leader doesn't have to know everything. But he or she must know where to get the required knowledge. A great example might be outsourcing an accountant, lawyer, or web designer for your business. A successful leader doesn't need to know how to pay his taxes, but needs to know where to go to get good tax advice. A successful leader doesn't need to be a lawyer but only needs to know where to go to get good legal advice.

36. Persistence

Don't give up. Running a successful business takes effort, focus, concentration, wisdom, and energy. You must believe in yourself and your ideas, or you will quit when you face your first challenge. And if you don't succeed at everything, redeem your failure by learning from it.

37. Amazing Customer Service

Everyone loves good customer service. If you help your customers, they will stay loyal to your products / services. If you listen to your customers, you will gain insight into their needs. Perhaps you may find an opportunity.

38. Investments

The rest of this Self-Economics section will focus on investments. There are countless types of investments and ways to invest. They can make you money, but they also can rob you of your future. If done correctly, in accordance with the below recommendations, investing in your future is never a bad idea.

39. How Much to Invest

This is an individual number. Some finance experts say 10%, others 20% or 30%. I'm not going to give you a hard and fast rule for investing percentages. But I will recommend that you invest in things that you can touch. Things which exist only on paper or in a computer can disappear more quickly than your rental property.

I used to invest a very large percentage of my income. As a Special Forces Soldier I did not make a lot of money, but I made a steady income. In 2008, I *had used my salary to build up $500,000 in "safe" investments. Because of the greed of so many people and the evilness of banks and money lenders, my life's investments were cut in half during the financial crisis and I was only worth $250,000. A few years later, I put $50,000 into a mutual fund which the manager stole from and bankrupted. I lost it all. In a four-year period, I lost $300,000 via bad investments, the equivalent of about five years of salary. Ouch. That hurt. And the truth is, I have never recovered that money. It is gone. I don't say this to discourage you, but to warn you to be careful.*

40. If You Don't Understand What It Is, Then Don't Invest in It

This is a great rule. Invest only in products you understand. If you don't understand how the fund or process works … then don't put your money into it. Do some research and come back later.

I knew what I was investing in, but lost over 50%. My heart goes out to the person who thought he was investing in something 100% safe and who loses his retirement and future.

There are a lot of investing options out there. Some of the most popular investments include cash or cash equivalents, bonds, CDs, your home, your pension, annuities, insurance, structured notes, equities, high-yield bonds, real estate, real estate investment trusts (REITs), commodities, currencies, collectibles … If you don't know what these are, then don't gamble with your future.[9]

41. Get a Fiduciary, not a Financial Planner

Many financial planners are great people doing the best they can. However, many are criminals and deceptive car salesmen. I recommend investing through a fiduciary rather than through a financial planner. A fiduciary is a financial planner who has agreed to provide more ethical and trustworthy investing assistance in the interest of making you money. Financial planners sell you funds and stocks, which make them money. Fiduciaries sell you what you need to be financially healthy.

42. Index Funds

You can't beat the market. Tony Robbins' *Money: Master the Game* reports that 96% of funds fail to outperform the market. This is a key point of his book. Rather than gamble with finding the perfect fund to invest in, people should simply invest in a low-fee index fund that mirrors the market, i.e., an S&P 500 fund.

---

[9] This list is from Robbins' *Money: Master the Game.*

43. Automate Savings & Investments

Automate your savings account. Ensure that you send a certain amount of your salary each month into your emergency savings account. Once you have decided to invest, set up your payments electronically so you don't have to think about it.

44. Minimize Fees

Mutual fund fees vary from 1-3%. Even a 1% fee can cost you hundreds of thousands of dollars over time. I recommend that you find an S&P market mirroring fund that has a 1% fee.

45. Roth IRA

A "Roth" Individual Retirement Account (IRA) allows you to pay taxes on the money you put into the investment, not the money you take out. Since, in theory, investments go up over time, you will be paying taxes on the lower amount that you put in while enjoying tax-free status on the larger amount that you pull out. The only catch is that you must be 59½ to begin pulling out your money tax free. So, if you can afford to invest and wait until you are 59½, then this is absolutely a great way to invest while minimizing taxes.

46. Roth 401(k)

Many employees invest in a 401(k) for retirement. What is even better is when an employer matches the employee's contribution, frequently up to 6% of their salary. For example, Jose makes $100,000 a year. He invests 6% of his salary ($6,000) a year into his 401(k). His employer matches that investment by also putting $6,000 a year into his 401(k). Jose invests only $6,000 a year, but actually has $12,000 in his 401(k). If your employer matches your 401(k) contributions, then you must max out what they will match. This is a simple way to instantaneously double your money.

Just as some investment funds are better than others, you need to ensure that your 401(k) is invested into a good fund. I recommend a market mirroring (think S&P 500) fund with a 1% maintenance fee.

When possible, invest in a Roth 401(k). This will allow you to pay taxes on the small amount you put in rather than the large amount you take out.

Many times, you don't have any control over where your 401(k) is invested. But if you do have control, or if you have a good employer who listens to good advice, then I recommend you ensure your 401(k) is a good one.

Manners

Having manners and showing proper etiquette is the best way to demonstrate that you respect yourself and those you are with.

1. Definition / History

"Etiquette" is a derivative of the French word for "ticket" or "label." By having etiquette, you are labeled as being from a good family, having a good education, and being approved to be seen in good circles, ultimately being able to be seen in court. By not having etiquette, you are labeled as having bad manners and being undedicated, or vulgar. Etiquette has also evolved into a description of proper behavior. If you have proper behavior, then you must be from a good family, have a good education, and are approved to be seen in good circles.

Every culture has their formal or informal rules for manners and etiquette. "Spanish Etiquette" is the most formal of Western systems of etiquette and is the system adopted and used by most of the European royalty.

2. Golden Rule

Do to others what you would want others to do to you (Matthew 7:12). This is a good rule by which to work and live.

3. Say Please & Thank You

Saying "please" and "thank you" is an essential way to demonstrate manners. If you can't remember to say "please" or "thank you," then flawlessly executing every other concept in this document is simply a waste of time.

4. Asking to Help

Able-bodied men should always ask if they can help women or the elderly. It is also good manners to ask other men if you can help. This goes for "moving day" or for simply carrying groceries up the apartment staircase. Men should always carry anything for a woman or the elderly. Men take out the trash, carry luggage, and carry groceries. Only if alone should a woman carry such things. Show manners by always asking to help.

5. Authenticity

People can tell if you don't care or are a faker. So be authentic, be real. No one can be the best at everything, so feel free to admit that you don't know something or can't do something. Don't pretend to care or be interested if you are not. Others will appreciate and respect your honesty.

6. Remember Names

You should remember almost everyone you meet, but especially people who are introduced to you. Among other things, remembering someone's name shows that you care. People with good manners do not make excuses for "not being good with names," but show people respect by remembering their names. People will notice and be appreciative.

7. Punctuality

Being on time illustrates that you are in control of your life and schedule, and it shows others that you respect their time. Because we have so many technological gadgets for keeping time and maintaining a schedule, there is no excuse for being late. Being punctual demonstrates that you can be taken seriously and that you keep your promises.

8. Greetings

If someone says, "Hello," or "Good afternoon," then it is required that you respond appropriately. It is never acceptable to ignore a greeting.

9. Introductions

It is always good manners to make a proper introduction. The introducer first addresses the "higher-ranking person" and then introduces the "lower-ranking person." For example: "Madam President, I would like to introduce my younger brother to you."

10. Never Interrupt

Cutting people off, ignoring them, not letting someone finish what they want to say, or not paying attention because you are formulating what you are going to say next are ways to burn bridges, destroy rapport, or lose a heart and mind.

11. Listening

People with manners are great listeners. They actively listen, ask engaging questions, and learn from the people around them.

12. Ask if it is Convenient for Others

Before you decide to involve someone else, verify the convenience of your decision with that person. For example, tell your sister that you would like to come for a visit and ask when would be a good time. Don't just tell her you are coming and give her the dates. Ask your apartment building neighbor when would be a good time to have your smoke detectors inspected. Don't just schedule a day which works best for you.

13. Communications and Vocabulary

People with manners are effective communicators. They know proper grammar and use languages elegantly. They know how to use and how to read body language and other nonverbal communications. Cussing and vulgarity are never acceptable.

14. Handshakes

A strong, firm handshake with eye contact is a good way to introduce yourself or conclude a matter. It shows respect for yourself. Be a bit gentler when shaking hands with a lady, but still be strong and firm. Only shake hands with a "higher-ranking person" if they offer you their hand. Flaccid handshakes are never appropriate.

15. Eye Contact

Eye contact is always appropriate. It is disrespectful to look around, look for other people, or look at your cell phone during a conversation.

16. Cell Phones

You must master your cell phone; do not let your cell phone master you. Use it appropriately, but don't let it get the best of you and your time. Don't talk on a cell phone in public. But if you must, be quiet and discreet. It is rude to be on the phone in line at the supermarket. It is very rude to be invited to someone's house and then check your cell phone frequently while there. It is rude to use your phone during dinner, even if you are at your own house. Show the hostess or cook respect by giving them, not your phone, your undivided attention. Using cell phones in your car has killed thousands of people. Please be careful and use hands-free devices in an automobile.

17. Holding Doors

Men should hold doors for women and the elderly. This is for buildings, houses, and vehicles. Brothers should open doors for their sisters so when they grow up they will expect nothing less. Women should slightly slow down when approaching a door to give the man enough time to open the door.

18. Walking in the Street

Couples: In days of old, a man would walk with the lady on his left, by his sword (also on his left hip), so he could use his right hand to draw and use his sword in their protection. Now, the rule is that a lady should walk on the safe side and a man on the dangerous side. Usually, the safe side is the outside of a street and the dangerous side is the side closest to the traffic. As you progress through town, you may need to switch sides to keep the lady on the safe side. Switch sides once safely on the sidewalk. If approaching parked cars or shady-looking men, then change sides as appropriate.

Professional / Military: The higher-ranking person walks on the right and the lower on the left. When a lower-ranking person needs to pass a higher-ranking person, the lower passes on the left and should say, "By your leave."

19. Vehicles

You can show manners in a vehicle or while driving. Obeying all traffic rules and paying attention to the road, not your cell phone, is a great way to show respect to others. And when it occurs that two people arrive at the same parking spot at the same time, use the "golden rule" and let the other person have it. Be generous and patient when driving. No one likes to drive with or around angry drivers, and the horn is the exception, not the rule.

20. Public Places

When in public places or on public transportation, priority for seating should always go to women and the elderly.

21. Invitations to Someone's House

RSVP when invited. Be punctual or a few minutes early. Never go anywhere empty-handed. Always bring a gift. Feel free to be generous. Bring a nice bottle of wine, some flowers, chocolate, a book ... Or bring a gift for the inviter's children. If you can't afford a gift, then make something or write a very nice thank-you note and give it to the inviter when you arrive. You can write a thank-you note after the event. But for most events, a verbal "thank you" before leaving the house is sufficient.

22. Restaurants

★ Invitations: If you "invite" someone to eat at a restaurant, then it is implied that you will pay. Make reservations, if possible, and be punctual or a few minutes early.

★ Couples: Once you enter the restaurant, the man walks first and the lady follows. The man seats the lady and then sits down himself. When dinner is over, the man can help the lady with her chair and with her jacket and handbag if needed, then the man walks out first and the lady follows. They can walk side by side or hold hands as soon as they reach the boundary of the restaurant.

★ Ordering: A man should always ask what the lady will eat and if she would like him to order for her. A man should order for himself and his lady.

- ★ Paying: Needless to say, the man should always pay when dining with a lady. If dining in a large group, even if you were invited, it is good manners to ask the inviter if you can pay for your share of the dinner.

23. Dining Table

- ★ Position: The highest-ranking man should always sit at the head of the table and get first choice of the main dish.

- ★ Prayers: Let the highest-ranking man offer the prayer. He may delegate the prayer if he so wishes.

- ★ Accessories: Women can wear hats while dining. Men must never wear hats while dining. Cell phones should not be used while dining.

- ★ Utensils: The general rule is that as the courses arrive, you will use the outermost utensils and work your way in. Use in pairs (fork and knife) if you are in doubt. A good hostess or waiter will bring you another knife if you used one prematurely.

- ★ Napkins: When you sit down, you may put your napkin on your lap. Always place your napkin with your left hand. After a meal, fold your napkin and place it on the table.

★ Finished Signal: Once you have finished a plate, place your utensils together with the tips at the center of your dish and the handles at the four o'clock position.

★ Leaving the Table: If you must leave the table early, then ask the host to be excused.

24. Posture

Having good posture shows respect. Having good posture is an essential ingredient for overall body health and is a good way to show others that you respect them and yourself. Good posture is also a good indicator of self-esteem.

25. Style & Grooming

The nicer you are dressed, the better you feel. Show respect for your host, colleagues, friends, and family by looking good and being well groomed. Shorts and a t-shirt are great for restful days at home, but are inappropriate for invitations and public places.

26. Always Exceed Expectations

If you are expected to deliver "one," exceed expectations and deliver "two." If you are required to give a presentation at the office, give the presentation, but exceed expectations and prepare snacks and beverages. By always exceeding expectations, you will enhance your reputation and show respect to others.

27. Send a Handwritten Thank You

In today's tech savvy world, people have forgotten their manners and how to write a nice letter. A handwritten letter is the most privileged form of read communication. Sending an email is satisfactory, but for the important messages of life, take the time to write it by hand. Always send a handwritten thank-you note when you receive a gift or an invitation. I recommend taking a few minutes each week to make a list of the people who helped you the most, the people who are working the hardest for you, or the people who need the most encouragement. Then write each one of them a quick note.

28. Email Standard Operating Procedures (SOP)

★ Email is a form of Communication / Not the Product: Many people are slaves to their emails. Effective people are "effective" because they are competent and make things happen, not because their email inbox is always empty and they have responded to every single email.
★ No Emotions: Keep all emails professional. Never get aggressive on email. If you need to

confront someone, be courageous and do it face to face.
- ★ To/CC/BCC Rules: If your name is in the "To" line, then you need to read the mail and perhaps a response or some work is required. If your name is in the "CC" or "BCC" line, then the email is just for your information.
- ★ Signature Blocks: If you are communicating with someone important, then always have a professional signature block with contact information.
- ★ Keep Records: If something may get contentious, then coordinate it over email so you have a written record with dates and times.
- ★ Leadership by Email: There is no such thing as leadership by email. So, communicate via email a few hours a day at the maximum, then leave your desk and lead.
- ★ Pick and choose. Ignore or delete unimportant emails. Perhaps block them. Respond to important emails and then move on.

29. Ask for Help

Pride comes before the fall. So, never think you are too wonderful to ask for help. People with manners are always learning, growing, developing, asking questions, and asking for help. A few good questions and a point in the right direction may save you time and money.

30. Wash Hands

It is rude to use the toilet and leave without washing your hands.

31. Scratching

It is rude to scratch your genitals in public.

32. Snorting or Spitting

It is rude to snort or spit in public. It is rude to wipe your nose with anything other than a tissue, Kleenex, or handkerchief. It is rude to clean your sinuses onto the ground in public. You should always use a tissue, Kleenex, or handkerchief.

33. Confidence

Confidence is always appreciated. Arrogance is never appreciated. Real confidence comes from the quiet certainty of one's abilities and proficiencies. False confidence comes from an overrated and unrealistic opinion of oneself and one's skills. People with manners and self-respect are all confident.

34. Humility

Humility is an essential attribute of someone with manners and is a result of the before mentioned quiet certainty of one's abilities and proficiencies. People with manners like to let their actions speak for themselves. They stay and remain grounded and humble.

35. Truth & Integrity

The truth will set you free. People with manners and self-respect don't have time for tangents or lies. They only tell the truth. People with manners have integrity and respect themselves and others.

Persuasion

Persuasion and influence are essential elements of effective communication. Understanding and mastering elements of persuasion ensures that your message is conveyed and your thoughts are communicated. All things being equal, the person who is a better persuader will win the debate. Although some people are naturally better communicators than others, with deliberate preparation and rehearsing, everyone can be more persuasive.

1. Persuasion -v- Manipulation

Persuasion is effective and influential communication to clarify and give meaning. Manipulation is Machiavellian and potentially unethical. Use persuasion to be understood, never to manipulate or deceive.

2. Elements of Persuasive Design

Elements of persuasive design help you to better understand and frame your persuasion opportunity. Using the below listed elements of persuasive design helps you to know what persuasive techniques you should use.

3. Authenticity / Winning Hearts and Minds

When fighting a war or competing in the marketplace, it is essential that you win the hearts and minds of the populace. You must show the people that you care for them and are there for them. Authenticity is a must. Honesty and integrity are essential. The audience is not dumb. They can spot an inauthentic faker a mile away. Don't pretend to care or be interested if you are not. Others will appreciate and respect your honesty.

4. KIS: Keep it Simple

The best way to be understood is to keep your message simple. A Harvard professor might teach you ten concepts in one class. A minister might have only three points to his sermon. A commercial only wants you to do one thing, buy their product. The simpler the message, the easier it is to remember.

5. Know your Purpose

What is the purpose or goal of your discussion, advertisement, briefing? What is the one "takeaway" you want your audience to understand?

6. Consider and Know your Audience

Knowing your audience is an essential element for persuasive design. Is it your boss, the CEO, a neighbor, the judge?

★ Who is the audience?
★ Are they prejudiced? Open for new ideas?
★ What do they think of me, my idea?
★ What do they value, know, have?
★ In what ways are they influenceable?

7. Have a Goal for Every Meeting / Engagement

Purposeless meetings / discussions / briefings are a waste of your precious time and energy, so stop them or stop going to them. If you do go to a meeting, know what you want to do or accomplish before every meeting starts. For example, "The goal of this meeting is to convince the Ambassador that we can accomplish this counter drug mission and that she should let us do it." Or "The goal of this meeting is to introduce our product to the customer and give them literature about how wonderful it is. We will wait two weeks and then ask them to purchase our product during our next meeting with them at their headquarters."

8. Emotional Intelligence

Being appropriately kind or assertive opens doors for communication. Most people shut down or get defensive when someone is aggressive or confrontational towards them. Using your emotional intelligence to better understand the mood and responsiveness of your audience will help make you more persuasive.

9. Don't Waste Your Time

Persuasion in a given time period has limits. Generally, you can only move one person one block at a time. (See below.) For example, someone who is "neutral" can be moved to be "supportive." But someone who is "very against" is unlikely to ever be "very supportive." Don't waste your time trying to convert the unconvertible. Spend time persuading those who potentially could become supporters. The butcher will never become a vegetarian. The Senator will never vote for the other party. Spend your time wisely to maximize results.

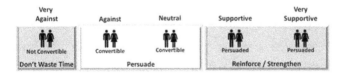

10. Rehearse, then Re-Rehearse

Rehearsals are an essential step in mission accomplishment. Once you have identified your persuasive tools, it is essential that you practice them. Rehearse your speech. Practice your timing. Make sure your body language is precise. Be prepared. Practice makes perfect.

Tools / Techniques of Persuasion

1. Appeal to Emotions

Some people think with their hearts. You must win over their heart before you can win them over.

2. Data and Statistics

Quote or reference hard data or statistics which support your argument. Some audiences love and only consider data. Others fear it. Know your audience and use statistics wisely.

3. Authority

Reference or quote a book, speaker, leader, famous person. Piggyback off their authority. Be associated with their authority.

4. Time / Resources are Scarce

A shortage of time and resources make us all jump into decisions. "Time is running out so buy now." "This is the last one in the store so buy now." "Be the first one in your neighborhood to have this."

5. Multimedia

Use multiple media to persuade. Create the appropriate emotional environment through sound, smell, images, video, or music.

6. Language and Vocabulary

Persuaders are effective communicators. They use grammar and languages appropriately.

7. I'm Just Like You (Language / Accent)

Speak with a "twang" or accent if that will help communicate your message. Use culturally appropriate language and references.

8. I'm Just Like You (Situation)

Emphasize how you are similar to the audience and that they can trust you, learn from your mistakes, or follow your example.

9. Ask Great Questions

The difference between a Harvard professor and a student professor at the local community college is that for sure the Harvard professor knows how to ask the right question to bring forth knowledge from the student. Persuaders ask the right question at the right time.

10. Body Language / Nonverbals

Great persuaders know how to use and how to read body language and other nonverbal communications.

11. Shock Factor

Make a bold declaration or take your argument to the most logical extreme.

12. Assume the Moral High Ground

Assume that the audience wants to take the moral high ground, and then associate that high ground with your position.

13. Ultimate Good

Explain how your position supports the ultimate good. People believe they are fair and unselfish. Use this apparent "fairness" to your advantage.

14. Illustrations

Give a great example or story which uses similar logic. Then circle back to your position.

15. Analogies

An analogy is a "resemblance in some particulars between things otherwise unlike."[10] For example, "just as the Earth needs the Sun to give it heat and light, students need their Philosophy teacher to give them wisdom and logic. Please don't take away the Sun from the Earth… or wisdom and logic from our students. We must keep funding the Philosophy department."

16. Metaphors

"A figure of speech in which a word or phrase literally denoting one kind of object or idea is used in place of another to suggest a likeness or analogy between them (as in 'drowning in money')."[11]

---

[10] https://www.merriam-webster.com/dictionary/analogy
[11] https://www.merriam-webster.com/dictionary/metaphor

17. Similes

"A figure of speech comparing two unlike things that is often introduced by like or as (as in 'cheeks like roses')."[12]

18. Humor

Use emotional responses to humor to make your point.

19. Likability

Although some audiences only care about the facts, most audiences become more agreeable if you are nice. This is related to using your emotional intelligence and being authentic.

20. Remember Names

You should remember almost everyone you meet. Persuaders remember names and lives. Among other things, remembering someone's name shows that you care. People will notice, and be more agreeable.

---

[12] https://www.merriam-webster.com/dictionary/simile

21. Give a Lot

Be generous and give, give, give. Then when it is time to persuade, your audience is more agreeable.

22. Foot in the Door

Getting your foot in the door means someone can't shut the door. So, if you can get them to agree on a part of your argument, then you can always go back to that point and try other techniques.

23. Say "Yes"

Ask your audience a question to which the answer is always "yes." Get them saying "yes" to these types of questions and then work your way towards your desired idea. Generally, people don't like to change their minds. Getting them to say "yes" once they have already said "no" is almost impossible. It becomes a matter of pride and self-esteem, not truth, logic or reality. Get them saying "yes" and never let them say "no."

24. Pride

Challenge someone to do great things. Brag about them. Use their pride and ambition against them.

25. Repetition

Repeat your point or phrase or argument over and over so that the audience can't forget it.

26. Persistence

Persistence is trying over and over again. Perhaps the fourth or fifth time they hear your message, they will be persuaded.

27. Storytelling

Never underestimate the power of a captivating story. Make it personal and emotional for even more effect.

28. Peer Pressure / Conformity

Most people will do anything to fit in. Highlight how everyone is doing it.

29. Duty

Remind the audience that it is their duty.

30. Fear

Link your argument to a potential threat or consequence of inactivity.

31. Take the Other Side

Take a break from your argument to discuss the other side. Pretend to advocate the other side, but highlight holes and logic gaps.

32. Alliterations / Rhymes

Make your point memorable through an alliteration or a rhyme: "70 SOF Skills for Success."

Negotiations

We all negotiate. Some more than others. Some negotiate terms and conditions every day of their professional lives. Other simply use negotiation skills when buying a car or establishing a cell phone contract. Nonetheless, everyone can benefit from improving their negotiation skills.

Lessons Learned from my Harvard Negotiations Course

I got an A (an A-) in my Negotiations Course while going to graduate school at Harvard. That particular year at Harvard cost me $63,000, and I took ten courses. So roughly speaking, my Harvard Negotiations Course cost me $6,300. The biggest lesson learned during that course was that 90% of your time must be used in the Pre-Negotiation Phase. The more you think about, plan for, rehearse, and re-rehearse your negotiation, the better the outcome.

Lessons Learned during Executive-Level Government Negotiations

Although I only got an A- in my Harvard Negotiations Course, I got an A+ during my time as a U.S. Army Special Forces (Green Beret) Lieutenant Colonel. I give myself this grade because after conducting countless negotiations on behalf of the security interests of the U.S. Government, I am still alive, and many bad guys are no longer terrorizing the world or selling and transporting illegal drugs.

Elements of Negotiation

The below listed elements of negotiation help frame a negotiation, keep us organized, and give us a common vocabulary which we can reference to speed up learning. Using the below listed elements of negotiation will help you to plan, prepare for, rehearse, and re-rehearse your negotiations.

1. Pre-Negotiation Phase

This is the preparation phase; 90% of your time must be spent in the Pre-Negotiation Phase. This is where you learn the details, gain competency, study your opponent, rehearse and re-rehearse. The more time you spend in the Pre-Negotiation Phase, the more likely you will have a successful outcome. Knowledge is king. The smartest and most competent person in the room always has the upper hand.

2. Negotiation Phase

This is the actual negotiation. This may be a formal and planned negotiation or it may be an informal negotiation during a chance encounter with a colleague or boss. Negotiation Phase considerations should be planned during the Pre-Negotiation Phase. If possible, it is best to plan for the negotiation with respect to time and location.

★ Time: Considerations for the time of your negotiation include knowing when you are at your best and when your opponent is at his worst. Possibly you have observed that your boss is not a morning person, so it takes her an hour to get going in the morning. Then schedule an early meeting to negotiate your new salary. Perhaps your boss is always happiest after a lunchtime workout. Then schedule the salary negotiation after her lunchtime workout.

★ Location: Pick a place where you feel well, or perhaps a place which proves your point. For example, if your work environment is counterproductive but the boss has an amazing office, schedule the salary negotiation in your terrible office cubicle so she can see how your work conditions are not optimal and that you deserve better compensation. Conduct the negotiation at the power plant so the CEO smells, feels, and lives the conditions of the workers.

3. Post-Negotiation Phase

The negotiation doesn't end when an agreement is made. Based on the outcome, you must write contracts, speak with lawyers, send apologies, brief subordinates, and write thank you letters. It is best to plan for Post-Negotiation Phase activities while still in the Pre-Negotiation Phase.

4. Define Your Objective

What is the purpose or goal of your negotiation? What do you want? Need? An easy example to better understand the "objective" is when negotiating for your salary at a new job. You may define your objective as $7,000 a month.

5. Define Your Minimum / Maximum

What is the minimum / maximum that you would settle for before cancelling the negotiation? In the example where your objective for a salary is $7,000 a month, you may decide that your minimum is $5,000. If you can't get $5,000 a month, then you walk away.

6. Currency & Value Come in Many Forms

A negotiation may be about one currency, a currency which has value. But there are almost always other currencies and values at work. A great negotiator identifies and understands all currencies and values at play.

For example, salary negotiations are very common. The amount of money (Currency 1) is usually the only currency discussed. But the reason we value money is that it pays the bills (Value 1) and buys us a better quality of life (Value 2). This better quality of life may mean taking time off (Currency 2) or eating higher quality food (Currency 3) and drinking more delicious, yet expensive, coffee (Currency 4) at the local coffee shop. We have now identified 4 Currencies to use at the negotiation table. Perhaps we can ask for a higher salary, and once that Currency is negotiated, you can ask for more vacation days (Currency 2), that the boss provides his employees with free, healthy snacks (Currency 3) and a new coffee machine with premium coffee beans (Currency 4). Now you may not have gotten the "Objective" salary, but you get more paid time off, free snacks, and better coffee. Congratulations, you won the negotiation.

7. Know and Understand all Parties

Frequently a negotiation is with one opposing party, or one person. For example: your boss, the CEO, a neighbor, the judge, or an ambassador. But other times a negotiation may involve many interested parties. For example: a homeowner's dispute between the city council, a construction company, the homeowner's association, and multiple homeowners. Knowing all the parties involved is an essential element of a negotiation.

★ Who are the parties involved?

- ★ Any allies? Threats?
- ★ What are their objectives?
- ★ What are their minimums / maximums?
- ★ Are they prejudiced? Open to new ideas?
- ★ What do they think of me, my position?
- ★ What do they value?
- ★ In what ways are they influenceable?

8. ZOPA

The Zone of Possible Agreement (ZOPA) is the entire range of negotiable currencies and values. The company may agree to pay an employee $4,000 to $6,000 a month. Your minimum is $5,000 a month, but your objective is $7,000. The ZOPA is $5,000 to $6,000. Many people go into a negotiation unprepared, not knowing the ZOPA. By doing your research during the Pre-Negotiation Phase, you might learn the ZOPA, giving you a better chance of maximizing your value. By knowing the ZOPA for this example, we see that your Objective of $7,000 a month is off the table ... but you can still negotiate up to $6,000 a month.[13]

---

[13] e.g. means *"exempli gratia"* or *"for example"*

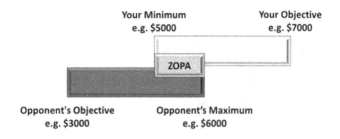

9. BATNA

The "Best Alternative to a Negotiated Agreement," or BATNA,[14] is what you will do if the negotiation fails. For example, you have enough money in the bank to pay off your bills for six months. So, if the company you are negotiating with doesn't meet your minimum, you can walk away and still survive for six more months as you seek employment elsewhere. In this case your BATNA is strong. If you have a weak BATNA, then you might have to settle. But if you have a strong BATNA, you can be bold, demand the best. You have less to lose.

10. Ethics

Never lie or cheat or steal, in life or during a negotiation. Stay ethical and always take the moral high

---

[14] BATNA and ZOPA are found in thousands of pieces of literature so I am defining them, rather than referencing the original work.

ground. Chances are your opponent will recognize your integrity and respect you for it.

11. Establish Negotiation Rules

When you first meet during a negotiation or even during the Pre-Negotiation Phase, it is wise to agree upon rules for the negotiation. For example, you will allow you opponent to present his argument for topic one (currency), then you present your argument. Each side has five minutes. Then you will move on to topic two, then three, and finally topic four. Then you get to make the first comprehensive negotiation, and your opponent can rebut. Establishing negotiation rules helps keep the negotiation on schedule.

12. Emotional Intelligence

Being appropriately kind or assertive opens doors for communication. Most people shut down or get defensive when someone is aggressive or confrontational towards them. Using your emotional intelligence to better understand the mood and responsiveness of your opponent will help make you more persuasive.

13. Body Language / Nonverbals

Great negotiators know how to use and how to read body language and other nonverbal communications.

14. Obstacles and Dead Ends

There are many obstacles and dead ends when negotiating. A completely unreasonable opponent is an obstacle or perhaps even a dead end. A very emotionally involved negotiating party may also be an obstacle. You should always plan for obstacles and dead ends during your Pre-Negotiation Phase activities.

15. Rehearse, then Re-Rehearse

Rehearsals are an essential step in the Pre-Negotiation Phase. Rehearse your speech or your presentation on applicable data. Practice your timing. Make sure your body language is precise. Be prepared. Practice makes perfect. Ask a colleague or friend to play the role of your opponent. Switch roles so that you are now the opponent. This may give you insights concerning their objectives and minimums. Like all skills, the more you practice negotiating, the better you will become.

Negotiation Tools / Techniques

1. Anchor Points

An anchor point is when you tentatively agree on something and decide to come back to it. If this agreement is better than your BATNA, establish that point as an anchor point. Then continue with your negotiation. If all else fails, you can return to your anchor point. It is likely that once you have an anchor point in place, you can work to find an even more agreeable solution.

2. High Initial Offer

If given the opportunity, you should make a high initial offer., perhaps even higher than your maximum. In the small chance that your opponent agrees, you have exceeded your maximum. If they counter, perhaps they will create value within your ZOPA.

3. Split the Difference

Human tendency is to split the difference. The math is easy and superficially seems fair. If your opponent offers 10 and you counter with 20, then likely you will agree on 15. But if your opponent offers 10 and you counter with 40, then splitting the difference brings you to 25. If you counter so as to split the difference, then make sure you calculate properly so that splitting the difference brings you to an agreeable value.

4. Role Play

If negotiating in a team, one person can be the "good guy" and another the "aggressive guy." Assign roles and stay in them during the negotiation.

5. Build Coalition

Like in war, negotiating in a coalition brings strength, resources, and legitimacy. When participating in a multiple-party negotiation, build a coalition as best that you can.

6. Let Other Parties Fight It Out

Sometimes it benefits you to let other interested parties fight it out before you get involved in a negotiation. If their coalition is humbled or they have shown their unprofessional side, it is possible that you can benefit from not being in the initial argument.

7. Appeal to Emotions

Some people think with their hearts. You must win over their heart before you can win them over.

8. Use Data and Statistics

Quote or reference hard data or statistics which support your argument. Some audiences love and only consider data. Others fear it. Know your audience and use statistics wisely.

9. Time / Resources are Scarce

A shortage of time and resources make us all jump into decisions. "Time is running out, so agree now." "This is the last one on the market, so agree now."

10. Bureaucracy

Let them know you are not authorized to "go that far" or that "to go that far" you will need some time to go through the proper bureaucratic approval process. Warning: honesty is always the best policy, so only say this if it is true. Second warning: if your opponent sees that you are not a decision maker, they may insist on rescheduling the negotiation with the actual decision maker.

11. Shock Factor

Make a bold declaration or take your argument to the most logical extreme. Then agreeing on something less severe seems reasonable.

12. Take the Other Side

Take a break from your argument to discuss the other side. Pretend to advocate the other side, but highlight holes and logic gaps.

13. Ultimate Good / Fairness

Explain how your position supports the ultimate good and is reasonable and fair. All people you meet think they are fair and unselfish. Take advantage of their apparent fairness and appeal to the nobler motive.

14. Give Away / Concede

Be generous and give away or concede less valuable currencies. When it is time to gain the real value from your primary currency, your opponent may be more agreeable. Plan ahead and know in advance which currencies and values you are going to give away.

15. Look for the Win / Win

This requires an honest discussion about value and currency with a trustworthy opponent. Perhaps you can make value for your opponent while gaining value for yourself.

Security

Elite Performers keep themselves, their loved ones, their property, their businesses, and their intellectual property secure. Now more than ever, we must be deliberate to maintain security. We will discuss security in three parts. The first part will be physical self-defense. Next, we will address the mindsets and habits of security. And the final portion of our discussion on security will involve practical steps you can make to protect your business and property.

Keeping yourself safe is more about making good decisions and less about fighting. It is a dangerous world out there. Please use your brain and keep safe.

1. Physical Self-Defense

You must master the basics before you start learning a fancy martial art. The basics are the front hand jab, the rear hand punch, the hook, the front kick, and the round kick. When people get into an emergency situation, they sometimes panic and only remember their basic instincts to punch and kick. This is why it is essential to master the punch and kick by having great technique, speed, and placement.

Elite Performers must know how to defend themselves and their loved ones. Learning self-defense is fun, practical, and builds confidence. We are proud to sponsor <u>Special Operations Fitness</u>, which has ten self-defense sessions. These self-defense workouts focus on basic boxing and kicking techniques and are guaranteed to "wear you out." Whether an experienced warrior or an amateur soccer mom, you will benefit from these challenging and confidence-building workouts.

2. Yell for Help

Someone may hear you yelling and come to help you. Yelling may scare off our opponent because he may think that help is on the way. Also, when you yell your opponent instinctively wants to put his hands on your mouth to quiet you. This give you a slight advantage because you at least know that his attention and hands are up high, near your face. He is not watching or prepared for a kick to the groin or knee.

3. The 120% Rule

The 120% rule is about speed and intensity. When you are defending yourself, give 120% and you will gain the advantage. We learn the 120% rule from cats. A cat weighs seven pounds. A human weighs 150 pounds. Yet when a man grabs a cat and the cat wants to be let loose, the cat will strike with their front paws so fast and so many times that a human, despite being twenty times bigger and stronger, always lets the cat go. The cat scratch doesn't cause permanent damage, but it hurts and startles you just enough that you reactively let the cat go. If a rapist is harassing you, then hit him in the face twenty times in five seconds, and for sure he will take a step back and reevaluate his life decisions.

4. Go for the Vulnerable Parts (Eyes, Throat, Groin)

If your life is being threatened, then don't hesitate to counterattack your opponent's most vulnerable places. Stick your fingers or thumbs into their eye sockets. Punch them in the neck until they can't breathe. Kick them in the testicles until they fall over. If someone wants to rape you, then don't feel bad about making them suffer or lose an eye.

5. Upgrade Your Situation

In Special Forces School, we are taught to always upgrade your situation by using what is near and available. Being hit by a fist hurts. Being hit by an iron hurts even more. But being hit by a hammer hurts even more. Being hit by a baseball bat hurts even more. Being hit by a car hurts even more. Do you understand my point? Everything has potential to be used as a weapon in your protection. See what is around you and use it. Upgrade your situation.

6. Avoid Bad Places

Bad things always happen at bad places. For example, I love the taste of Bailey's Irish Cream. But I enjoy this beverage from my house, where I am safe and sound, while I am reading a book and getting smarter. There is no way that I would order a shot at the local Irish pub or the local motorcycle bar. Loud music, hormones, and alcohol are the three ingredients of stupidity. Avoid dumb places and keep yourself safe.

7. Low Profile

Being a success is much better than being famous. Being famous makes you a target. By keeping a low profile in life, you make yourself less of a target and avoid opportunities where you may need to defend yourself. If no one knows who you are, they are less likely to hate you and want to hurt you.

8. Don't Flash Your Wealth

Bad guys prefer lucrative targets or targets of opportunity. Flaunting your wealth may cost it. Hide your watch and handbag when you are in a bad neighborhood. Staying invisible is the best way to avoid a dangerous situation.

9. The Two-Man Rule

Bad guys are less likely to bother two people than a single one. It is always safer to have a buddy or chaperone.

10. The Ten p.m. Rule

Nothing good ever happens away from your house after ten p.m. Period. Stay home and remain safe. Teenagers and knuckleheads hate this rule, but it is true. Stay home and remain exponentially safer.

11. Safety Gear

Statistics tell us that safety gear works. Yes, there are a few exceptions. But for the most part, it is always best to wear your seatbelt, wear a helmet, hearing protection, eye protection, and gloves. Having lived a dangerous lifestyle for decades, I can't tell you how many times over my safety gear has paid for itself by keeping me alive and in one piece. For example, at one point in my life I had seven helmets (a bulletproof helmet for my body armor, a skateboard helmet, a snowboard helmet, a road bike helmet, and a mountain bike helmet, a sky diving helmet and a motorcycle helmet). I packed my own parachute, but always had a reserve. I wear my seatbelt and only recently stopped riding a motorcycle. I have caught myself on fire, been in flight in a helicopter that caught on fire, got stuck underneath a moving boat, and have been hit by a shark. This list doesn't even include what happened to me while deployed to war zones. Safety gear works and I highly recommend that you buy the best gear available.

12. Cyber Security

Elite Performers have an aggressive cyber security plan. For decades, Special Forces Operators have communicated from behind enemy lines using passwords, secure voice and data communications, and other unconventional communication techniques. In modern times, cybersecurity is no longer just for governments, military and business professionals. Cyber security is for everyone.

We live our lives online and from computers more and more each day. Many people spend the majority of their "working" hours in front of a computer. Whether you are a student or a web designer, an engineer or a CIA agent, everyone must learn and master the basics of cyber security.

13. Antivirus

You must protect your computer and devises from viruses. Many antivirus programs are free. Most are inexpensive. And almost all of them are effective against most threats. I recommend that you use a reputable and inexpensive antivirus. The second part of the antivirus equation is to not open email or attachments from unknown senders and do not click on attachments or links which are out of context. If you don't know who sent you the email, don't open it. If it was important, they would have called. If you know the sender but the attachment or hyperlink is sketchy, call the sender and ask them about it.

14. Back Up Your Data

I don't recommend that you backup your data online. Online data clouds are less secure than a backup hard drive stored in the fireproof safe hidden behind a shelf in your subterranean nuclear fallout bunker. All kidding aside, backing up your data to an external hard drive once a week means that if your computer crashes you lose a week's worth of work, not all your work.

15. Passwords

A complex password is exponentially more secure than a simple password. Use a phrase or song lyrics or anything complex and random to secure your online identity. Don't use the same password for every account. Everyone knows this rule, but many are too lazy to do it.

16. VPN

A Virtual Private Network (VPN) allows you to be on the internet without anyone collecting information on you. A good VPN doesn't cost very much and can help you maintain a smaller internet footprint. In 2019, I pay $3 a month for my VPN and I can use it from my smart phone, tablet, and computer. Although most people have nothing to hide, all of us can benefit from greater privacy.

17. Social Media Privacy

Several popular social media outlets delete what you post after a few days. Some never save what you post. And others maintain ownership of what you post forever. Regardless of what social media outlets you use, I recommend that you read their terms of usage and adjust what you post accordingly. Remember, what you post can and will be used against you.

18. Car Security

Always lock your car. This goes for when you are driving, as well. Never leave valuables in your car. If you must leave valuables in your car, then cover them or place them where they are not visible. Park your car in a visible location. The car in the back of the parking lot is the one that gets robbed. So, park up front if and when you can. Don't go to a dark parking garage by yourself. If it is late at night or dark, ask someone you trust to walk you to your car. Don't forget the ten p.m. rule or that two is better than one. Keep some pepper spray in the door panel of your car and in your purse.

19. House Security

Although entire books are written about home security, I want to give the executive summary of the best ideas I have used and taught throughout my life.

Always lock your doors and windows. Fake cameras and alarm company signs are good defenses against amateurs. Real cameras and real alarms are even better. For a few hundred dollars, you can buy and install a security camera system which you can view from your smart phone via the internet. For a few thousand dollars, you can have a professional install an alarm system, and security company surveillance fees range from a hundred to a thousand dollars a year, depending on the package and the response time you require. Don't hide keys anywhere near your door. If you must hide a key, make it very hard to get and find. When you are on a long vacation, I recommend that you make it appear as if you are at home by asking someone to collect your mail and newspaper, and by setting a few of your lights on timers. Build a symbiotic relationship with your neighbors regarding home security. If they know that you aren't moving, then they will call the police when a moving truck pulls up to your house while you are on vacation. Motion detectors are great ways to scare off potential intruders. Keep pepper spray or a weapon near the door in case you actually have an intruder. Rehearse evacuation routines and fire drills.

20. Smart Phone Security

Unsecured smart phones are stolen all the time. It hurts to have your thousand-dollar smart phone stolen. But it hurts even more when the thief has access to your bank account, investments, Amazon, social media profiles, and private photos. I recommend that you always lock and password protect your smart phone. I further recommend that you use some type of "locate my smart phone" application and share it with someone you trust. If you think of your smart phone as a one-thousand-dollar bill, you are less likely to set it on the table or forget it at the coffee shop.

21. Emergency Fund

You must have an emergency savings account. When your car needs new brakes or when your washing machine dies, it is important that you pay for it in cash, out of your emergency savings account. If you don't have an emergency savings account, then you will pay for the brakes or new washing machine with a credit card. This will only give you more debt.

I recommend that your emergency savings account is at least:
- ★ $2 thousand (hotel money for a week if you must fly to a funeral)
- ★ plus $1 thousand for each family member living in your household (emergency airline tickets)
- ★ plus $2 thousand for each house you own (money to fix or replace an appliance)
- ★ plus $1 thousand for each vehicle your family owns (major vehicle repair)

For example, a family of five with three cars and one house has an emergency savings fund of $12 thousand. I hope you never must use your emergency fund, but statistically speaking, you will one day fly the entire family home for a funeral.

I also recommend that you stash a bit of cash as appropriate in random places. I always keep a hundred dollars in the glove box of my car so I can fill my gas tank or take my wife for "emergency sushi" date night. I tape a hundred-dollar bill behind my passport cover. I put a twenty in my mountain bike bag in case I need an emergency ice cream while exercising.

22. Emergency Kit for the Car

Keep an emergency kit in your vehicle's trunk that includes water, food (something like power bars or granola bars), a small tool kit, a small first aid kit, jumper cables, a flashlight, a rain jacket, a warm jacket, a few dollars, a reflective triangle, and a Leatherman or multi-tool.

23. Emergency Kit for the House

Depending on the size of your family, the length of an anticipated disaster, and the level of your paranoia, I recommend that every household has some variation of an emergency kit at home. A big storm may destroy the power grid for a few days. Or perhaps the government doesn't balance the budget and government employees don't get paid for a month or two. For sure your home emergency kit must have a few working fire extinguishers, a first aid kit, candles, batteries, food, and water. Perhaps a bee sting kit. Perhaps a water purifier. If you know how to cook, you can make a million items from good flour and olive oil. These items are cheap and easy to stockpile. In the event that your electricity goes out for a long time, feast on the items in your refrigerator, which will go bad first. Use your gas or charcoal barbeque to make the most of your tragedy. Plan ahead, and life during a crisis will be much more bearable.

24. Intelligence

It is always a good idea to know what your "competition" is up to. Knowledge about your competition is called intelligence. In peace time and war, most governments use spies to gather intelligence. Elite Performers simply need to listen to the news, read the internet, and pay attention to world events.

25. Counterintelligence

Preventing your "competition" from learning about you and your business is called counterintelligence. An active counterintelligence program includes protecting your proprietary business models and ideas, your computer systems, bank information, and personal identification information.

Conclusion: Do What You Know is Right

The last idea I leave with you is: "Do What You Know is Right."

Although many of these Elite Performance Skills are common sense or easy to understand, mastering them and making them a part of your day-to-day habits is not an easy process. The key is to do what you know is right.

Everyone knows that soda is bad for you. Yet millions of fat people drink them every day. A hundred percent of Americans will tell you that, in theory, having a budget and a financial plan is a good idea. Yet, half of them don't have a budget and live with constant credit card debt.

The key to success is to do what you know is right. I am honored to have shared with you so many principles of success. But reading these Elite Performance Skills alone is not enough. <u>You must do them. You must study them, rehearse them, and make them your own.</u>

Because Elite Performers plan everything, it is now time for you to start planning the next phases of your life. As with many Special Operations, real life is hard to execute. There will be challenges. There will be setbacks. But the rewards are enormous and the view from the top of the mountain is worth every step you took to get there. If you study, train, rehearse, and master all these Elite Performance

Skills, then nothing will keep you from success. I congratulate you in advance.

Now get to work!

Copyright © 2019 by Littlestone

All rights reserved. No part of this publication may be reproduced, distributed or transmitted in any form or by any means, without prior written permission.

Elite Performance Skills / Paperback -- 1st ed.
ISBN: 978-1-946373-04-5
$17.99 everywhere great books are sold

CPSIA information can be obtained
at www.ICGtesting.com
Printed in the USA
BVHW081404130521
607269BV00011B/2149